THE BEST OF
JAMES
WHITCOMB
RILEY

THE BEST OF
JAMES
WHITCOMB
RILEY

Edited by DONALD C. MANLOVE

*INDIANA
UNIVERSITY
PRESS
Bloomington*

First Midland Book Edition 1982
Introductory material and notes
copyright © 1982 by Donald C. Manlove

Manufactured in the United States of America

Library of Congress Cataloging in Publication Data

Riley, James Whitcomb, 1849-1916.
    The best of James Whitcomb Riley.

    Includes index.
    1. Manlove, Donald C.   II. Title.
PS2702.M36 1982   811'.4   82-47958
1 2 3 4 5 86 85 84 83 82

CLOTH ISBN 0-253-11060

PAPER ISBN 0-253-20299-X

Contents

[vii]

Sketches in Prose

EDITOR'S PREFACE

The best of Riley. What criteria have been used in making the selection?

My first concern has been to give a balanced picture of the whole range of Riley's work. Riley wrote poems, he wrote prose pieces, he wrote one play. He wrote in dialect and in standard English. He wrote humorous pieces and serious pieces, poems for children and poems about children for adults. Riley's mentor, Captain Lee O. Harris, and the poet Riley loved best, Henry Wadsworth Longfellow, counseled him to write about what was closest to his heart. He followed their advice and discovered gold in the dark, rich soil of Indiana. His poems celebrate everyday life and everyday people and the everyday glories of a beautiful place. "I will sing of black haws, Mayapples, and pennyroyal; of hazel thickets, sycamores, and shellbark hickories in the pathless woods." Greenfield was his town, Indiana was his state, America was his country, and the magical world of children everywhere was his special province.

The Best of Riley includes all the poems and pieces that fall into any one of three categories that frequently overlap: the poems most frequently anthologized, Mr. Riley's particular favorites, and the favorites of the editor, who has been engaged in interpreting Riley's works for over forty years. The poems are in chronological order; the year of composition for each (from *The Biographical Edition of James Whitcomb Riley*, edited by Edmund H. Eitel [Indianapolis: Bobbs-Merrill, 1912]) is given on the Contents pages.

The illustrations are by Will Vawter—like Riley, a native of Greenfield—who illustrated many of Riley's books and did a series of paintings of Greenfield scenes for Marcus Dickey's two-volume biography of Riley.

I have enjoyed putting this volume together. I hope it brings the reader untold hours of satisfaction and enjoyment.

Donald C. Manlove

JAMES WHITCOMB RILEY was born on October 7, 1849, in a log cabin in the village of Greenfield in Hancock County, Indiana. He was the third of six children born to Reuben Alexander and Elizabeth Marine Riley. John Andrew was the eldest, followed by Martha Celestia (who died in early childhood), then "Bud" (as James was often called), Elva May (seven years younger than Bud), Humboldt Alexander (who had several nicknames—Hum, Alex, Alec) and Mary, the baby of the family, who was often called "Lizzie."

Riley's mother, Elizabeth Marine Riley, descended from English Quakers and French Huguenots, was born in North Carolina in 1823. In 1825 her parents moved west to Indiana and settled by the Mississinewa River in Randolph County. Her father was a flat-boat builder, a miller, a preacher (he and his wife led many Methodist camp meetings in Randolph and Delaware counties), and a poet. "John Marine wrote his autobiography in rhyme," said his famous grandson. "He would sit by the fireplace and write heavy turbid poetry on scientific and Biblical subjects. The tendency was to the epic."* His daughter Elizabeth was also a poet. Her chief delight in childhood, according to an old friend, "was to play along streams and wander in the green woods." A Greenfield neighbor described Mrs. Riley as "the most patient woman I ever knew, deeply sympathetic, indulgent to a fault," who "rarely addressed her children in other than endearing terms."† She loved to tell her children fairy tales, funny stories, and stories of her own childhood. One of her favorites was about her meeting and talking with Johnny Appleseed, who told her that "growing old in Heaven is growing young," which became her own lifelong vision of Heaven. She wrote rhymes and skits for her children and encouraged them to make up their own; they frequently put on "shows" and "circuses" for their friends. She was deeply loved by all her children, but she and Bud were especially close. When she died suddenly in 1870, her oldest child, John Andrew, wrote in his diary, "What shall we do with Jim now that mother is dead?†

*Quoted material is from Marcus Dickey's two-volume biography of Riley: *The Youth of James Whitcomb Riley* (Indianapolis: Bobbs-Merrill, 1919) and *The Maturity of James Whitcomb Riley* (Indianapolis: Bobbs-Merrill, 1922), except that marked with a dagger, which is from Minnie Belle Mitchell, *James Whitcomb Riley as I Knew Him* (Greenfield, Indiana: The Old Swimmin' Hole Press, 1949).

Her husband, Reuben A. Riley, of Irish, German, and English descent, was born in Pennsylvania in 1819. His family moved to western Ohio in 1825 and a few years later to Randolph County, Indiana, where "they lived on the fat of the land," said family tradition. There was plenty of game—red deer, wild turkey, and black bear were abundant in the rich primeval forest—and cleared land was extraordinarily fertile—gardens and crops grew well. Reuben Riley and Elizabeth Marine were married in 1844 and in that same year moved to Greenfield, which was then 15 years old, where Reuben Riley opened a law office. He was very active in the affairs of the town and the county—he was the first mayor of Greenfield, and he was elected to represent Hancock County in the state legislature. An orator of considerable ability, he was much in demand as a speaker at political rallies. His political opinions were strongly held. He was a Democrat until the Fremont campaign, when he became a Republican. He was proud that he was a delegate-at-large to the Chicago convention that nominated Abraham Lincoln for President, and when the war came, he went through the county recruiting men to fight for the Union. The company he formed was the first in the state to be accepted by the governor, who gave him a captain's commission. Reuben Riley shared his wife's love of nature and liked to teach his children the names, habits, and uses of the abundant flora and fauna of the Indiana countryside. He was a gifted craftsman, who took pleasure in making everything from the finest stilts and kites in town to a chair that had in it every kind of wood that grew in the county. He built the spiral staircase of black walnut (still in existence in the restored Riley homestead in Greenfield) that figures in the story "Where Is Mary Alice Smith?" (p. 190 in this volume), and when Bud was still quite small, his father made him a suit with a fashionable long-tailed cutaway coat like that of Judge Wick, the friend and colleague whose law office adjoined Reuben Riley's.

Few boys have had a happier childhood than James Whitcomb Riley. Greenfield in Riley's boyhood was a community of approximately 300 souls. The texture of daily living was rich, and that wealth is cherished and beautifully inventoried in Riley's poems and stories. Pioneers and the children of pioneers, the people of the village were accustomed to being self-reliant, so each had many skills; at the same time neighbors and neighborliness were far more important to the people of Greenfield than they were to those who lived in the older towns of the East. Together the people of Greenfield were building a community; each person's special skills were needed and valued. People were busy at home and next door and a few doors down—in the garden and the orchard and the barn, at the cobbler's and the blacksmith's, at the courthouse and the mill—and children were part of it all. Boredom was never a problem, although there was often strong resentment over having to hoe the garden or shovel manure when a boy would far rather be swimming or fishing in the Brandywine or stealing watermelons or playing Indians in the woods or watching the antics of his new pet raccoon. And a child could have a fine time just watching the road, for Greenfield, while largely self-sufficient, was by no means isolated. The main street was the Old National Road, the brainchild of Geoge Washington, who saw clearly the need for it and campaigned to have it built. It was the main, and for many years the only, road from the East to the western frontiers. Riley was born the year gold was discovered at Sutter's Mill. Through Greenfield over the years streamed the thousands upon thousands going west to stake their claim in the gold fields or on the prairies. They came in wagons, in carts, in "prairie schooners," with pack trains, on foot, on horseback. They brought news and travelers' tales and kept Greenfield steadily supplied with novelty, amusement, excitement, and revenue. From his earliest childhood Bud was an excellent mimic, quick to notice the odd and unusual and exploit it for comic effect, and at his front door there was a never-ending cavalcade of fascinating characters.

School (which was, to the great satisfaction of the children, at least sporadic—it was not always easy for the parents to find, or afford, a teacher) was mostly a torment to the young Riley. He often played hooky and was often punished for it. As his friend Bill Nye said, "The lad got his education by listening to the inculcation of morals and then sallying forth with other lads to see if Turner's plums were ripe." Arithmetic was a mystery, a misery, and a torture; history bored him. Schools and most schoolbooks he hated, but to the schoolmaster of his teenage years, Captain Lee O. Harris, who became a lifelong friend, he owed, said Riley, "possibly the first gratitude of my heart and soul, since, after a brief warfare, upon our first acquaintance as teacher and pupil, he informed me gently but firmly that since I was so persistent in secretly reading novels during school hours he would insist upon his right to choose the novel I should read, whereupon the Beadle and Munro dime novels were discarded for masterpieces of fiction." Another important influence was Tom Snow, an Englishman who had been a member of London literary clubs and possessed a vast knowledge of English authors. Dickens was his favorite author, and Tom Snow brought a full set of Dickens' works to Greenfield. He came to Greenfield to farm but when he found he could grow nothing but calamus on the swampy land that was his, he set up a shoe-shop and later established himself in a bookstore that was "a headquarters for all sorts and conditions of village life, particularly for young fellows inclined to reading."

Around 1850 a New Harmony philanthorpist had given Greenfield a library of 300 volumes, the McClure Township Library. It included the works of Washington Irving, Prescott's histories, Cooper's novels, Macaulay's history of England and "a full line of the poets." At first the library was housed in the county courthouse, but it later drifted to the schoolhouse, then to Tom Snow's shoe-shop. The library, said Riley's biographer Marcus Dickey, "was a Mecca for young Riley. . . . His taste ran to fiction and poetry. . . . In the Township Library Riley . . . found the *Life of Daniel Boone,* the *Swiss Family Robinson, Don Quixote, Robin Hood, Robinson Crusoe,* and what was to him dearest of all, the *Arabian Nights.* . . . But the leaven from the library, the most generative and far-reaching in its effect was *The Lives of Eminent British Painters and Sculptors,* five leather-bound volumes with a long title, which . . . was simplified for talking purposes. 'Where's Riley?' someone asked. 'Oh,' answered an old-timer, 'he's up there readin' them British books.' " In the history of the artists' sorrows, struggles, and successes Riley found hope and inspiration that helped him through the discouraging years ahead, the years when his father and many others in Greenfield and sometimes Jim himself wondered what he was ever going to make of himself, the years of rejection letters from the newspaper and magazine publishers to whom he sent his poems.

Riley left school when he was sixteen. He wrote poems, played in the Adelphian Band, amused his friends with his impersonations, acted in parlor theatricals, went to dances, hung out in the shoe-shop with his friends reading and talking about books and life with Tom Snow, discussed literature with Captain Harris, drew pictures, and painted houses for pocket money. He had so many interests and talents that it was hard for him to concentrate on any one of them. At one point he resolved to become a concert violinist and began practicing long hours every day. But an injury to his thumb ended that dream. He was generally underfoot and at loose ends. His father was just home from the war, which had taken its toll, on both his health—he was injured in the battle of Rich Mountain—and his law practice, much of which drifted to other lawyers during his four-year absence from Greenfield; he wished Jim would study law but to ensure that he would at least learn *some* way of making a living, paid for his apprenticeship to a sign painter.

In January 1870 a new Academy opened in Greenfield. Riley attended for a short while but his marks were disastrous. In the spring he went to work for Tom Snow, but Tom died soon after and the shop was closed. He spent the fall of 1870 (a sad time for him—his mother had died suddenly in August) selling Bibles door to door in the Rushville area. 1871 found him back in Greenfield, where he set up shop as a sign-painter. In 1872 a traveling medicine show, Dr. McCrillus' Standard Remedies, came to town. When it left, Riley was part of it. He painted the advertising placards, did any other odd bit of art that was needed, and sometimes delivered comic recitations from the back steps of the wagon. "The Bear Story" was a crowd-pleaser from the first time he told it. Working for the medicine show was not much more rewarding financially than the sign-painting shop had been, but it was certainly more interesting. The show traveled all over Indiana and to some parts of Ohio. He left the show in 1873; that summer he and a fellow veteran of Dr. McCrillus' show traveled through Indiana painting advertising on barns. They eventually added another couple of partners and called themselves The Graphic Company. Their home base was Anderson; from there they traveled throughout the state, painting signs, playing practical jokes, and generally making life livelier wherever they went. They enjoyed themselves—sometimes. When they made money, they spent it. When they couldn't find work, they suffered; more than once they had to resort to sneaking out of town under cover of darkness because they had no money to pay the hotel keeper. On one memorable occasion the hotel keeper was similarly plagued by debts; he left town with Riley. "Together we moved furniture and all to Huntington [from Marion], drove in a wagon through the rain thirty miles—and through the night, too."

In the spring of 1874 Riley's father persuaded him to read law. But of the hours he spent in his father's quiet little office, probably more were spent in daydreaming and writing poems than in reading Blackstone and Coke. In the spring of 1875 two important events happened: Riley received his first check for a poem, and a medicine show, the Wizard Oil Company, came to town. Riley was off on his travels again, painting signs and entertaining the folks with his recitations. "Farmer Whipple, Bachelor" and "Dot Leedle Boy" were among his favorites. When the Wizard Oil tour ended in the fall, Riley became the local editor of his home paper at no pay and in a few months (in his own words) "strangled the little thing into a change of ownership." The new owner made him literary editor and he filled the allotted space with his verse. By now other Indiana newspapers were publishing his poems. In April of 1877 he was hired to edit the Anderson *Democrat*, a weekly paper. For the first time in his life he was under contract at a regular salary—$40 a month. By the end of his first month the circulation had doubled, and his salary was raised to $60. In four months' time the circulation of the paper had risen from 400 to 2400, and papers throughout Indiana were commenting on Riley's work—some were even pirating it. "Country correspondents scarcely recognized their prosy items, after they had passed through the 'humorous mill'. . . . It was said that [Riley] 'could coax more laughter out of an ink bottle into the *Democrat* than any two papers in the state could hold.'" Then one night he and a number of his practical-joke-playing old friends planned the "Leonainie" hoax. All through the seventies Riley had been submitting poems to Eastern newspapers and magazines and receiving only rejection letters for his pains. In later years, reminiscing about his struggle to be published, he said, "I remember two years that were just protuberant with hopeless days. I had the longest face between Toronto and Tehuantepec." Riley contended that the publishers' criterion was not the merit of the poem but the fame of its author, that only the work of established authors had any chance. He decided to prove his point. He wrote a poem, "Leonainie," in the style of Poe. It was printed in the Kokomo *Dispatch* (whose editor was one of those in on the secret) with a trumped-up story that led readers to believe it was a long-lost work by Poe. "Leonainie" was reprinted in newspapers all over the country, and men of letters debated whether the poem was in fact Poe's work. When the truth was revealed, Riley was subjected to a barrage of furious condemnation. He left the *Democrat* and Anderson and went home to Greenfield deeply chagrined. Even many years later, "Leonainie" was still a sore subject; when asked about it, Riley would say, "I'm reminded of the farmer who was asked about his legal troubles. 'Wa'al, I was arrested for stealing shoats,' he said, 'and the wust of it wuz, the prosecution come durn near provin' it.'"

The aftermath of the "Leonainie" affair, a nadir for Riley, in fact marked the turning point in his career. His success at the *Democrat* and the furor over the deception had made him well-known. Midwestern papers were eager to publish his work. The Indianapolis *Journal* offered him a job, and from then on he had a regular outlet for his work and a steady salary.

It was the age of the Chautauqua movement, of the lecture platform and the speaking tour. During the eighties, Riley became one of its brightest stars. As early as 1875, encouraged by the success of his recitations in the medicine show, he had begun to give solo programs of his poetry and stories. The small turnout at his first few readings was disheartening, but he persisted, paying careful attention to audience reaction, revising pieces and learning how to shape and pace the program, which always included both serious and comic pieces. From his early readings he learned (as he advised a young writer many years later) that "[an audience] never tires of simple, wholesome, happy themes. . . . An audience is cosmopolitan in character, a neighborly gathering, all on a level. The rich are there, and they are interested in the poor, since they came originally from the ranks of those who walk by the wayside. They know as I know that the crude man is generally moral, for Nature has just let go his hand. She's just been leading him through the dead leaves and the daisies. When I deal with such a man in my readings, I give him credit for every virtue; but what he does and the way he does it is *his* way, not mine. It is my office to interpret him.

"I talk of the dear old times when there were no social distinctions, of pioneer homes and towns, where there was a warm welcome for all, just as if all were blood brothers as Kipling says. I muse or romp happily amid the scenes of my childhood and the paradise is promptly recognized and appreciated by my audience."

By the late seventies his hard work and careful study of other speakers and actors had borne fruit; he was much in demand around the state. In 1879 he added to his program a lecture called "Poetry and Character." It began with praise of his favorite poet, Longfellow, for "spontaneity of expression and the grace of pure simplicity," and went on to an eloquent defense of dialect poetry. "The nearer the approach to nature, in language, expression, and unobtrusive utterance, the higher the value of Character and Poetry." To illustrate his point he read "Farmer Whipple — Bachelor" and "An Old Sweetheart of Mine." Like Robert Burns, whose poetry he loved, Riley wrote of and for the common people. In his dialect poems, said Marcus Dickey, Riley "rescue[d] from oblivion the disappearing vernacular of the frontier and the thought of an age in Indiana that was fast passing away."

The 1880s were a decade of intense, sometimes hectic, activity for Riley. The poems poured forth at a remarkable rate—in one three-year period he wrote over 300 poems. He would seclude himself for days, sometimes weeks, at a time and emerge with a sheaf of new poems. He was supplying not only the *Journal* but also a number of other papers with poems and prose sketches. Between bouts of writing he gave readings. His fame rapidly spread throughout the Midwest and beyond. Lecture bureaus were eager to sign him up. In 1882 he toured New England. Appearing in Boston, where his hero Dickens had been so enthusiastically received on his American tour thirteen years before, was thrilling to him, as were his meetings with editors and authors he had long corresponded with, including

Longfellow, whose praise and encouragement meant a great deal to him. Audiences loved him. "Never any other man," wrote Booth Tarkington, "stood night after night on stage or platform to receive such solid roars of applause for the reading of poems and for himself. He did not 'read' his poems; he did not recite them, either; he took his whole body into his hands, as it were, and by his wizard mastery of suggestion left no James Whitcomb Riley at all upon the stage; instead the audiences saw and heard whatever the incomparable comedian wished them to see and hear."

During the last half of the decade Riley was on tour virtually year round. The pinnacle of his platform career was his appearance in New York in 1887 at the invitation of the prestigious International Copyright League. James Russell Lowell introduced him to an audience of the most highly regarded authors, critics, editors, and publishers of the day. Riley recited "When the Frost is on the Punkin" and "The Object Lesson." These were so heartily appreciated that Riley was asked to make an unscheduled repeat appearance on the second day of the readings. He read "Nothin' to Say" with such tenderness that the same audience he had made helpless with laughter the day before was moved to tears. Sir Henry Irving, the famous actor and manager who dominated the English stage for more than thirty years, was in the audience and afterwards said, "The American stage lost a great actor when Riley refused to take the profession seriously as a life work."

By the end of the decade Riley's friends were concerned for him. The inevitable discomforts of life on the road were stressful, but even more stressful was the lecture bureau's exploitation of Riley. "In business affairs," Riley said, "a poet is as defenseless as a duckling." He had never been a good manager of money. In 1890 his brother-in-law Henry Eitel took charge of Riley's financial affairs, and they were handled very capably for the rest of Riley's life. But when the poet signed a five-year-contract with the Western Lyceum Agency in 1885, he had consulted no one. By the time of his last tour, Riley was being paid $40 an evening to give a program that usually brought in house receipts in excess of $1000. In January of 1890 Riley resolved that he would never again tour full-time. Thereafter he spent most of his time preparing manuscripts for publication.

For most lyric poets the time of greatest productivity comes early in their lives—the 1870s and 1880s were Riley's most prolific years. He had never thrown away anything he had written, and only a few volumes of his poetry had been published in the busy years of touring. There was a tremendous demand for his poetry, and there was a tremendous body of unpublished work. Riley set to work sorting, revising, grouping, arranging sequences, reading proof; each book represented many hours of hard work and agonized consideration and re-consideration of the selection and placement of the poems in it. Between 1890 and 1902, the years his biographer calls "the book-building period," eleven volumes of previously unpublished work appeared.

The nineties were a time of settling down in another way, too. During the previous two decades Riley had lived with friends or in boardinghouses in Indianapolis and Greenfield and Anderson, never staying in one place long, even when he was not on tour. His restlessness and the demands of touring were among the reasons he never married any of the sweethearts of his youth. To his friends he expressed his doubt that a poet, especially a traveling poet, would make a good husband. In his later years he remarked wistfully that when he found the girl he had no money and when he had the money he couldn't find the girl. By the time he was in his early thirties he had already learned, painfully, that total abstinence from alcohol was the wisest policy for him. His occasional lapses sorrowed him and may have been another factor in his decision not to marry. In 1893 he went to live as a paying guest in the home of his dear friends Major and Mrs. Charles L. Holstein on Lockerbie Street in Indianapolis; the Holsteins made it Riley's home as well as theirs. Riley lived there for the rest of his life.

Riley jokingly called the Lockerbie Street years "the venerable and time-honored epoch." He was rich and famous and his work was enormously popular. Wabash College, Indiana University, Yale University, and the University of Pennsylvania bestowed honorary degrees on him. Distinguished men of letters corresponded with him, visited him at Lockerbie Street, and praised him in print; struggling young writers sought his advice. His poems were printed in the prestigious Eastern magazines, such as the *Atlantic Monthly,* whose rejection letters had been the despair of his early career. William Dean Howells, the elder statesmen of the American literary establishment, called Riley "one of the greatest of our poets." Riley particularly treasured the praise and encouragement given him by Rudyard Kipling and Mark Twain.

In 1911 Riley suffered a stroke. For a while his death seemed imminent, but he soon rallied enough to enjoy the visits of friends and being driven around his beloved Indianapolis. (He once wrote, "When I die, I expect to wake right up again in Indianapolis, and though I have heard Heaven very highly spoken of, I will more than likely remark: 'Well, boys, you hain't overdrawn the pictur' ary particle.'")

In his remaining years there were many expressions of the public's affection for him. From 1911 onward Indiana schools had been celebrating his birthday, October 7, and in 1915 the governor of Indiana declared it Riley Day, as did the National Commissioner of Education, who directed that Riley Day be observed in all the schools of the United States. In Indianapolis a banquet was held in his honor. Four hundred people attended and hundreds more had to be turned away for lack of room. Riley received scores of congratulatory cables, including a message from President Woodrow Wilson, and was obviously very moved by the tributes to him.

Riley passed his sixty-sixth birthday in apparent good health. He spent the winter in Miami, Florida, as he had done for many years, and returned to Lockerbie Street well and happy. On July 22, 1916, he retired at his usual time and died in his sleep.

When his brother Hum died, Riley wrote, "He is not gone, he is just away." Perhaps James Whitcomb Riley is just away. His works are still with us, vibrant and alive.

THE BEST OF
JAMES
WHITCOMB
RILEY

A BACKWARD LOOK

Riley and his friend Clinton Hamilton launched a school paper called the Criterion. *On foolscap they printed by hand the school news as well as jokes, many of the latter written in rhyme by Riley, who also illustrated the paper. "A Backward Look" appeared in the second, and last, issue.*

As I sat smoking, alone, yesterday,
And lazily leaning back in my chair,
Enjoying myself in a general way—
Allowing my thoughts a holiday
   From weariness, toil and care,—
My fancies—doubtless, for ventilation—
   Left ajar the gates of my mind,—
And Memory, seeing the situation,
   Slipped out in the street of "Auld Lang Syne."—

Wandering ever with tireless feet
   Through scenes of silence, and jubilee
Of long-hushed voices; and faces sweet
Were thronging the shadowy side of the street
   As far as the eye could see;
Dreaming again, in anticipation,
   The same old dreams of our boyhood's days
That never come true, from the vague sensation
   Of walking asleep in the world's strange ways.

Away to the house where I was born!
   And there was the selfsame clock that ticked
From the close of dusk to the burst of morn,
When life-warm hands plucked the golden corn
   And helped when the apples were picked.
And the "chany dog" on the mantelshelf,
   With the gilded collar and yellow eyes,
Looked just as at first, when I hugged myself
   Sound asleep with the dear surprise.

And down to the swing in the locust-tree,
  Where the grass was worn from the trampled ground,
And where "Eck" Skinner, "Old" Carr, and three
Or four such other boys used to be
  "Doin' sky-scrapers," or "whirlin' round":
And again Bob climbed for the bluebird's nest,
  And again "had shows" in the buggy-shed
Of Guymon's barn, where still, unguessed,
  The old ghosts romp through the best days dead!

And again I gazed from the old schoolroom
  With a wistful look, of a long June day,
When on my cheek was the hectic bloom
Caught of Mischief, as I presume—
  He had such a "partial" way,
It seemed, toward me.—And again I thought
  Of a probable likelihood to be
Kept in after school—for a girl was caught
  Catching a note from me.

And down through the woods to the swimming-hole—
  Where the big, white, hollow old sycamore grows,—
And we never cared when the water was cold,
And always "ducked " the boy that told
  On the fellow that tied the clothes.—
When life went so like a dreamy rhyme,
  That it seems to me now that then
The world was having a jollier time
  Than it ever will have again.

THE OLD TIMES WERE THE BEST

Friends, my heart is half aweary
  Of its happiness to-night:
Though your songs are gay and cheery,
  And your spirits feather-light,
There's a ghostly music haunting
  Still the heart of every guest
And a voiceless chorus chanting
  That the Old Times were the best.

CHORUS

All about is bright and pleasant
  With the sound of song and jest,
Yet a feeling's ever present
  That the Old Times were the best.

"TRADIN' JOE"

I'm one o' these cur'ous kind o' chaps
You think you know when you don't, perhaps!
I hain't no fool—ner I don't p'tend
To be so smart I could rickommend
Myself fer a *congerssman*, my friend!—
But I'm kind o' betwixt-and-between, you know,—
One o' these fellers 'at folks call "slow."
And I'll say jest here I'm kind o' queer
Regardin' things 'at I *see* and *hear*,—
Fer I'm *thick* o' hearin' *sometimes*, and
It's hard to git me to understand;
But other times it hain't, you bet!
Fer I don't sleep with both eyes shet!

I've swapped a power in stock, and so
The neighbers calls me "Tradin' Joe"—
And I'm goin' to tell you 'bout a trade,—
And one o' the best I ever made:

Folks has gone so fur's to say
'At I'm well fixed, in a *worldly* way,
And *bein'* so, and a *widower*,
It's not su'prisin', as you'll infer,
I'm purty handy among the sect—
Widders especially, rickollect!
And I won't deny that along o' late
I've hankered a heap fer the married state—
But some way o' 'nother the longer we wait
The harder it is to discover a mate.

Marshall Thomas,—a friend o' mine,
Doin' some in the tradin' line,
But a'most too *young* to know it all—
On'y at *picnics* er some *ball!*—
Says to me, in a banterin' way,

As we was a-loadin' stock one day,—
"You're a-huntin' a wife, and I want you to see
My girl's mother, at Kankakee!—
She hain't over forty—good-lookin' and spry,
And jest the woman to fill your eye!
And I'm a-goin' there Sund'y,—and now," says he,
"I want to take you along with *me;*
And you marry *her,* and," he says, "by 'shaw!
You'll hev me fer yer son-in-law!"
I studied a while, and says I, "Well, I'll
First have to see ef she suits my style;
And ef she does, you kin bet your life
Your mother-in-law will be my wife!"

Well, Sund'y come; and I fixed up some—
Putt on a collar—I did, by gum!—
Got down my "plug," and my satin vest—
(You wouldn't know me to see me dressed!—
But any one knows ef you got the clothes
You kin go in the crowd wher' the best of 'em goes!)
And I greeced my boots, 'and combed my hair
Keerfully over the bald place there;
And Marshall Thomas and me that day
Eat our dinners with Widder Gray
And her girl Han'! * * *

               Well, jest a glance
O' the widder's smilin' countenance,
A-cuttin' up chicken and big pot-pies,
Would make a man hungry in Paradise!
And passin' p'serves and jelly and cake
'At would make an *angel's* appetite *ache!* —
Pourin' out coffee as yaller as gold—
Twic't as much as the cup could hold—
La! it was rich!—And then she'd say,
"Take some o' *this!*" in her coaxin' way,
Tell ef I'd been a hoss I'd 'a' *foundered,* shore,
And jest dropped dead on her white-oak floor!

Well, the way I talked would 'a' done you good,
Ef you'd 'a' been there to 'a' understood;
Tel I noticed Hanner and Marshall, they
Was a-noticin' me in a cur'ous way;
So I says to myse'f, says I, "Now, Joe,
The best thing fer you is to jest go slow!"
And I simmered down, and let them do
The bulk o' the talkin' the evening through.

And Marshall was still in a talkative gait
When he left, that evening—tolable late.
"How do you like her?" he says to me;
Says I, "She suits, to a 't-y-*Tee*'!"
And then I ast how matters stood
With him in the *opposite* neighberhood?
"Bully!" he says; "I ruther guess
I'll finally git her to say the 'yes.'
I named it to her to-night, and she
Kind o' smiled, and said *'she'd see'*—
And that's a purty good sign'" says he:
"Yes," says I, "you're ahead o' *me!*"
And then he laughed, and said, *"Go in!"*
And patted me on the shoulder ag'in.

Well, ever sense then I've been ridin' a good
Deal through the Kankakee neighberhood;
And I make it convenient sometimes to stop
And hitch a few minutes, and kind o' drop
In at the widder's, and talk o' the crop
And one thing o' 'nother. And week afore last
The notion struck me, as I drove past,
I'd stop at the place and state my case—
Might as well do it at first as last!

I felt first-rate; so I hitched at the gate,
And went up to the house; and, strange to relate,
Marshall Thomas had dropped in *too.*—
"Glad to see you, sir, how do you do?"
He says, says he! Well—it *sounded queer:*

[6]

And when Han' told me to take a cheer,
Marshall got up and putt out o' the room—
And motioned his hand fer the *widder* to come.
I didn't say nothin' fer quite a spell,
But thinks I to myse'f, "There's a dog in the well!"
And Han' *she* smiled so cur'ous at me—
Says I, "What's up?" And she says, says she,
"Marshall's been at me to marry ag'in,
And I told him 'no,' jest as you come in."
Well, somepin' o' 'nother in that girl's voice
Says to me, "Joseph, here's your choice!"
And another minute her guileless breast
Was lovin'ly throbbin' ag'in my vest!—
And then I kissed her, and heered a smack
Come like a' echo a-flutterin' back,
And we looked around, and in full view
Marshall was kissin' the widder, too!
Well, we all of us laughed, in our glad su'prise,
Tel the tears come *a-streamin'* out of our eyes!
And when Marsh said "'Twas the squarest trade
That ever me and him had made,"
We both shuck hands, 'y jucks! and swore
We'd stick together ferevermore.
And old Squire Chipman tuck us the trip:
And Marshall and me's in pardnership!

THE BEAR STORY

THAT ALEX "IST MAKED UP HIS-OWN-SE'F"

This had its beginnings in a story told by Riley's younger brother, Alex. In the early 1870s when Riley was traveling with Dr. McCrillus's Standard Remedies medicine show, an early version of "The Bear Story" was part of his recitation repertoire. Riley revised it over the years and frequently used it in his lecture program. What follows is the story as it first appeared in print in 1896. Country audiences knew that neither boy nor bear can climb a sycamore.

W'y, wunst they wuz a Little Boy went out
In the woods to shoot a Bear. So, he went out
'Way in the grea'-big woods—he did.—An' he
Wuz goin' along—an' goin' along, you know,
An' purty soon he heerd somepin' go *"Wooh!"*—
Ist thataway—*"Woo-ooh!"* An' he wuz *skeered*,
He wuz. An' so he runned an' clumbed a tree—
A grea'-big tree, he did,—a sicka-*more* tree.
An' nen he heerd it ag'in: an' he looked round,
An' *'t'uz a Bear!*—*a grea'-big shore-nuff Bear!*—
No: 't'uz *two* Bears, it wuz—two grea'-big Bears—

[8]

One of 'em wuz—ist *one'z a grea'-big* Bear.—
But they ist *boff* went "*Wooh!*"—An' here *they* come
To climb the tree an' git the Little Boy
An' eat him up!

An' nen the Little Boy
He 'uz skeered worse'n ever! An' here come
The grea'-big Bear a-climbin' th' tree to git
The Little Boy an' eat him up—Oh, *no!*—
It 'usn't the *Big* Bear 'at clumb the tree—
It 'uz the *Little* Bear. So here *he* come
Climbin' the tree—an' climbin' the tree! Nen when
He git wite *clos't* to the Little Boy, w'y nen
The Little Boy he ist pulled up his gun
An' *shot* the Bear, he did, an' killed him dead!
An' nen the Bear he falled clean on down out
The tree—away clean to the ground, he did—
Spling-splung! he falled *plum'* down, and' killed him, too!
An' lit wite side o' where the *Big* Bear's at.

An' nen the Big Bear's awful mad, you bet!—
'Cause—'cause the Little Boy he shot his gun
An' killed the *Little* Bear.—'Cause the *Big* Bear
He—he 'uz the Little Bear's Papa.—An' so here
He come to climb the big old tree an' git
The Little Boy an' eat him up! An' when
The Little Boy he saw the *grea'-big Bear*
A-comin', he 'uz badder skeered, he wuz,
Than *any* time! An' so he think he'll climb
Up *higher*—'way up higher in the tree
Than the old *Bear* kin climb, you know.—But he—
He *can't* climb higher 'an old *Bears* kin climb,—
'Cause Bears kin climb up higher in the trees
Than any little Boys in all the Wo-r-r-ld!

An' so here come the grea'-big Bear, he did,—
A-climbin' up—an' up the tree, to git
The Little Boy an' eat him up! An' so
The Little Boy he clumbed on higher, an' higher,

An' higher up the tree—an' higher—an' higher—
An' higher'n iss-here *house* is!—An' here come
Th' old Bear—clos'ter to him all the time!—
An' nen—first thing you know,—when th' old Big Bear
Wuz wite clos't to him—nen the Little Boy
Ist jabbed his gun wite in the old Bear's mouf
An' shot an' killed him dead!—No; I *fergot,*—
He didn't shoot the grea'-big Bear at all—
'Cause *they 'uz no load in the gun,* you know—
'Cause when he shot the *Little* Bear, w'y, nen
No load 'uz anymore nen *in* the gun!

But th' Little Boy clumbed *higher* up, he did—
He clumbed *lots* higher—an' on up *higher*—an' higher
An' *higher*—tel he ist *can't* climb no higher,
'Cause nen the limbs 'uz all so little, 'way
Up in the teeny-weeny tip-top of
The tree, they'd break down wiv him ef he don't
Be keerful! So he stop an' think: An' nen
He look around—An' here come th' old Bear!
An' so the Little Boy make up his mind
He's got to ist git out o' there *some* way!—
'Cause here come the old Bear!—so clos't, his bref's
Purt' nigh so's he kin feel how hot it is
Ag'inst his bare feet—ist like old "Ring's" bref
When he's ben out a-huntin' an's all tired.
So when th' old Bear's so clos't—the Little Boy
Ist gives a grea'-big jump fer *'nother* tree—
No!—no he don't do that!—I tell you what
The Little Boy does:—W'y, nen—w'y, he—Oh, *yes*—
The Little Boy *he finds a hole up there*
'At's in the tree—an' climbs in there an' *hides*—
An' *nen* th' old Bear can't find the Little Boy
At all!—But, purty soon th' old Bear finds
The Little Boy's *gun* 'at's up there—'cause the *gun*
It's too *tall* to tooked wiv him in the hole.
So, when the old Bear fin' the *gun,* he knows
The Little Boy's ist *hid* 'round *somers* there,—

An' th' old Bear 'gins to snuff an' sniff around,
An' sniff an' snuff around—so's he kind find
Out where the Little Boy's hid at.—An' nen—nen—
Oh, *yes!*—W'y, purty soon the old Bear climbs
'Way out on a big limb—a grea'-long limb,—
An' nen the Little Boy climbs out the hole
An' takes his ax an' chops the limb off! . . . Nen
The old Bear falls *k-splunge!* clean to the ground
An' bust an' kill hisse'f plum' dead, he did!

An' nen the Little Boy he git his gun
An' 'menced a-climbin' down the tree ag'in—
No!—no, he *didn't* git his *gun*—'cause when
The *Bear* falled, nen the *gun* falled, too—An' broked
It all to pieces, too!—An' *nicest* gun!—
His Pa ist buyed it!—An' the Little Boy
Ist cried, he did; an' went on climbin' down
The tree—an' climbin' down—an' climbin' down!—
An'-sir! when he 'uz purt'-nigh down,—w'y, nen
The old Bear he jumped up ag'in!—an' he
Ain't dead at all—*ist* 'tendin' thataway,
So he kin git the Little Boy an' eat
Him up! But the Little Boy he 'uz too smart
To climb clean *down* the tree.—An' the old Bear
He can't climb *up* the tree no more—'cause when
He fell, he broke one of his—he broke *all*
His legs!—an' nen he *couldn't* climb! But he
Ist won't go 'way an' let the Little Boy
Come down out of the tree. An' the old Bear
Ist growls 'round there, he does—ist growls an' goes
"*Wooh!*—*Woo-ooh!*" all the time! An' Little Boy
He haf to stay up in the tree—all night—
An' 'thout no *supper* neever!—On'y they
Wuz *apples* on the tree!—An' Little Boy
Et apples—ist all night—an' cried—an' cried!
Nen when 't'uz morning th' old Bear went "*Wooh!*"
Ag'in, an' try to climb up in the tree
An' git the Little Boy.—But he *can't*
Climb t'save his *soul,* he can't!—An' oh! he's *mad!*—

He ist tear up the ground! an' go *"Woo-ooh!"*
An'—*Oh, yes!*—purty soon, when morning's come
All *light*—so's you kin *see,* you know,—w'y, nen
The old Bear finds the Little Boy's *gun,* you know,
'At's on the ground.—(An' it ain't broke at all—
I ist *said* that!) An' so the old Bear think
He'll take the gun an' *shoot* the Little Boy:—
But *Bears they* don't know much 'bout shootin' guns;
So when he go to shoot the Little Boy,
The old Bear got the *other* end the gun
Ag'in' his shoulder, 'stid o' *th'other* end—
So when he try to shoot the Little Boy,
It shot *the Bear,* it did—an' killed him dead!
An' nen the Little Boy clumb down the tree
An' chopped his old woolly head off:—Yes, an' killed
The *other* Bear ag'in, he did—an' killed
All *boff* the bears, he did—an' tuk 'em home
An' *cooked* 'em, too, an' *et* 'em!
—An' that's all.

FARMER WHIPPLE—BACHELOR

It's a mystery to see me—a man o' fifty-four,
Who's lived a cross old bachelor fer thirty year' and more—
A-lookin' glad and smilin'! And they's none o' you can say
That you can guess the reason why I feel so good to-day!

I must tell you all about it! But I'll have to deviate
A little in beginnin', so's to set the matter straight
As to how it comes to happen that I never took a wife—
Kindo' "crawfish" from the Present to the Springtime of my
    life!

I was brought up in the country: Of a family of five—
Three brothers and a sister—I'm the only one alive,—
Fer they all died little babies; and 'twas one o' Mother's ways,
You know, to want a daughter; so she took a girl to raise.

The sweetest little thing she was, with rosy cheeks, and fat—
We was little chunks o' shavers then about as high as that!
But someway we sort o' *suited*-like! and Mother she'd declare
She never laid her eyes on a more lovin' pair

Than *we* was! So we growed up side by side fer thirteen year',
And every hour of it she growed to me more dear!—
W'y, even Father's dyin', as he did, I do believe
Warn't more affectin' to me than it was to see her grieve!

I was then a lad o' twenty; and I felt a flash o' pride
In thinkin' all depended on *me* now to pervide
Fer mother and fer Mary; and I went about the place
With sleeves rolled up—and workin', with a mighty smilin'
    face.—

Fer *somepin' else* was workin'! but not a word I said
Of a certain sort o' notion that was runnin' through my
    head,—

[13]

"Some day I'd maybe marry, and a *brother's* love was one
Thing—a *lover's* was another!" was the way the notion run!

I remember onc't in harvest, when the "cradle-in'" was done,
(When the harvest of my summers mounted up to twenty-
        one),
I was ridin' home with Mary at the closin' o' the day—
A-chawin' straws and thinkin', in a lover's lazy way!

And Mary's cheeks was burnin' like the sunset down the lane:
I noticed she was thinkin', too, and ast her to explain.
Well—when she turned and *kissed* me, *with her arms around
        me—law*!
I'd a bigger load o' Heaven than I had a load o' straw!

I don't p'tend to learnin', but I'll tell you what's a fac',
They's a mighty truthful sayin' somers in a' almanac—
Er *somers*—'bout "puore happiness"—perhaps some folks'll
        laugh
At the idy—"only lastin' just two seconds and a half."—

But it's jest as true as preachin'!—fer that was a *sister's* kiss,
And a sister's lovin' confidence a-tellin' to me this:—
"*She* was happy, *bein' promised to the son o' Farmer Brown.*"—
And my feelin's struck a pardnership with sunset and went
        down!

I don't know *how* I acted, and I don't know *what* I said,—
Fer my heart seemed jest a-turnin' to an ice-cold lump o' lead;
And the hosses kind o' glimmered before me in the road,
And the lines fell from my fingers—And that was all I
        knowed—

Fer—well, I don't know *how* long—They's a dim remember-
        ence
Of a sound o' snortin' horses, and a stake-and-ridered fence
A-whizzin' past, and wheat-sheaves a-dancin' in the air,
And Mary screamin' "Murder!" and a-runnin' up to where

I was layin' by the roadside, and the wagon upside down
A-leanin' on the gate-post, with the wheels a-whirlin' roun'!
And I tried to raise and meet her, but I couldn't, with a vague
Sort o' notion comin' to me that I had a broken leg.

Well, the women nussed me through it; but many a time I'd sigh
As I'd keep a-gittin' better instid o' goin' to die,
And wonder what was left *me* worth livin' fer below,
When the girl I loved was married to another, don't you
    know!

And my thoughts was as rebellious as the folks was good and kind
When Brown and Mary married—Railly must 'a' been my *mind*
Was kind o' out o' kilter!—fer I hated Brown, you see,
Worse'n *pizen*—and the feller whittled crutches out fer *me*—

And done a thousand little ac's o' kindness and respec'—
And me a-wishin' all the time that I could break his neck!
My relief was like a mourner's when the funeral is done
When they moved to Illinois in the Fall o' Forty-one.

Then I went to work in airnest—I had nothin' much in view
But to drownd out rickollections—and it kep' me busy, too!
But I slowly thrived and prospered, tel Mother used to say
She expected yit to see me a wealthy man some day.

Then I'd think how little *money* was, compared to happiness—
And who'd be left to use it when I died I couldn't guess!
But I've still kep' speculatin' and a-gainin' year by year,
Tel I'm payin' half the taxes in the county, mighty near!

Well!—A year ago er better, a letter comes to hand
Astin' how I'd like to dicker fer some Illinois land—
"The feller that had owned it," it went ahead to state,
"Had jest deceased, insolvent, leavin' chance to speculate,"—

And then it closed by sayin' that I'd "better come and see."—
I'd never been West, anyhow—a'most too wild fer *me*,

I'd allus had a notion; but a lawyer here in town
Said I'd find myself mistakend when I come to look around.

So I bids good-by to Mother, and I jumps aboard the train,
A-thinkin' what I'd bring her when I come back home again —
And ef she'd had an idy what the present was to be,
I think it's more'n likely she'd 'a' went along with me!

Cars is awful tejus ridin', fer all they go so fast!
But finally they called out my stoppin'-place at last:
And that night, at the tavern, I dreamp' I was a train
O'cars, and *skeered* at somepin', runnin' down a country lane!

Well, in the morning airly — after huntin' up the man —
The lawyer who was wantin' to swap the piece o' land —
We started fer the country; and I ast the history
Of the farm — its former owner — and so forth, etcetery!

And — well — it was inte*rest*in' — I su'prised him, I suppose,
By the loud and frequent manner in which I blowed my
       nose! —
But his su'prise was greater, and it made him wonder more,
When I kissed and hugged the widder when she met us at the
       door! —

It was Mary: . . . They's a feelin' a-hidin' down in here —
Of course I can't explain it, ner ever make it clear. —
It was with us in that meetin', I don't want you to fergit!
And it makes me kind o' nervous when I think about it yit!

I *bought* that farm, and *deeded* it, afore I left the town,
With "title clear to mansions in the skies," to Mary Brown!
And fu'thermore, I took her and the *children* — fer you see,
They'd never seed their Grandma — and I fetched 'em home
       with me.

So *now* you've got an idy why a man o' fifty-four,
Who's lived a cross old bachelor fer thirty year' and more
Is a-lookin' glad and smilin'! — And I've jest come into town
To git a pair o' license fer to *marry* Mary Brown.

DOT LEEDLE BOY

One of Mr. Riley's favorite public readings.

Ot's a lecdle Gristmas story
Dot I told der leedle folks—
Und I vant you stop dot laughin'
   Und grackin' funny jokes!—
So help me Peter-Moses!
   Ot's no time for monkey-shine,
Ober I vast told you somedings
   Of dot leedle boy of mine!

Ot vas von cold Vinter vedder,
   Ven der snow vas all about—
Dot you have to chop der hatchet
   Eef you got der sauerkraut!
Und der cheekens on der hind leg
   Vas standin' in der shine
Der sun shmile out dot morning
   On dot leedle boy of mine.

He vas yoost a leedle baby
   Not bigger as a doll
Dot time I got acquaintet—
   Ach! you ought to heard 'im squall!—
I grackys! dot's der moosic
   Ot make me feel so fine
Ven first I vas been marriet—
   Oh, dot leedle boy of mine!

He look yoost like his fader!—
   So, ven der vimmen said,
"Vot a purty leedle baby!"
   Katrina shake der head. . . .
I dink she must 'a' notice
   Dot der baby vas a-gryin',
Und she cover up der blankets
   Of dot leedle boy of mine.

Vel, ven he vas got bigger,
    Dot he grawl und bump his nose,
Und make der table over,
    Und molasses on his glothes—
Dot make 'im all der sveeter,—
    So I say to my Katrine,
"Better you vas quit a-shpankin'
    Dot leedle boy of mine!"

No more he vas older
    As about a dozen months
He speak der English language
    Und der German—bote at vonce!
Und he dringk his glass of lager
    Like a Londsman fon der Rhine—
Und I klingk my glass togeder
    Mit dot leedle boy of mine!

I vish you could 'a' seen id—
    Ven he glimb up on der chair
Und shmash der lookin'-glasses
    Ven he try to comb his hair
Mit a hammer!—Und Katrina
    Say, "Dot's an ugly sign!"
But I laugh und vink my fingers
    At dot leedle boy of mine.

But vonce, dot Vinter morning,
    He shlip out in der snow
Mitout no stockin's on 'im.—
    He say he "vant to go
Und fly some mit der birdies!"
    Und ve give 'im medi-cine
Ven he catch der "parrygoric"—
    Dot leedle boy of mine!

Und so I set und nurse 'im,
    Vile der Gristmas vas come roun',
Und I told 'im 'bout "Kriss Kringle,"

How he come der chimbly down:
Und I ask 'im eef he love 'im
    Eef he bring 'im someding fine?
"Nicht besser as mein fader,"
    Say dot leedle boy of mine.—

Und he put his arms aroun' me
    Und hug so close und tight,
I hear der clock a-tickin'
    All der balance of der night! . . .
Someding make me feel so funny
    Ven I say to my Katrine,
"Let us go and fill der stockin's
    Of dot leedle boy of mine."

Vell.—Ve buyed a leedle horses
    Dot you pull 'im mit a shtring,
Und a leedle fancy jay-bird—
    Eef you vant to hear 'im sing
You took 'im by der topknot
    Und yoost blow in behine—
Und dot make much *spectakel*
    For dot leedle boy of mine!

Und gandies, nuts und raizens—
    Und I buy a leedle drum
Dot I vant to hear 'im rattle
    Ven der Gristmas morning come!
Und a leedle shmall tin rooster
    Dot vould crow so loud und fine
Ven he sqveeze 'im in der morning,
    Dot leedle boy of mine!

Und—vile ve vas a-fixin'—
    Dot leedle boy vake out!
I t'ought he been a-dreamin'
    "Kriss Kringle" vas about,—
For he say—*"Dot's him!—I see 'im*
    Mit der shtars dot make der shine!"

Und he yoost keep on a-gryin'—
  Dot leedle boy of mine,—

Und gottin' vorse und vorser—
  Und tumble on der bed!
So—ven der doctor seen id,
  He kindo' shake his head,
Und feel his pulse—und visper,
  "Der boy is a-dyin'."
You dink I could *believe* id?—
  Dot leedle boy of mine?

I told you, friends—dot's someding,
  Der last time dot he speak
Und say, *"Good-by, Kriss Kringle!"*
  —dot make me feel so veak
I yoost kneel down und drimble,
  Und bur-sed out a-gryin',
"Mein Gott, mein Gott in Himmel!—
  Dot leedle boy of mine!"

. . . . .

Der sun don't shine *dot* Gristmas!
  . . . Eef dot leedle boy vould *liff'd*—
No deefer-in'! for *Heaven* vas
  His leedle Gristmas gift!
Und der *rooster*, und der *gandy*,
  Und me—und my Katrine—
Und der jay-bird—is a-vaiting
  For dot leedle boy of mine.

IF I KNEW WHAT POETS KNOW

If I knew what poets know,
Would I write a rhyme
Of the buds that never blow
  In the summer-time?
Would I sing of golden seeds
Springing up in ironweeds?
And of rain-drops turned to snow,
If I knew what poets know?

Did I know what poets do,
  Would I sing a song
Sadder than the pigeon's coo
  When the days are long?
Where I found a heart in pain,
I would make it glad again;
And the false should be the true,
Did I know what poets do.

If I knew what poets know,
  I would find a theme
Sweeter than the placid flow
  Of the fairest dream:
I would sing of love that lives
On the errors it forgives;
And the world would better grow
If I knew what poets know.

AN OLD SWEETHEART OF MINE

Written in Riley's father's law office in 1875. It was probably inspired by the poet's memories of Adda Rowell. When Riley was nineteen, tthe Rowell family, on their way from the East to settle in the Northwest, decided to break their long journey in Greenfield. They arrived in the spring and stayed until fall. The romance between Riley and Adda was shattered when her family moved on; Riley never forgot the winsome Adda.

An old sweetheart of mine!—Is this her presence here with
    me,
Or but a vain creation of a lover's memory?
A fair, illusive vision that would vanish into air
Dared I even touch the silence with the whisper of a prayer?

Nay, let me then believe in all the blended false and true—
The semblance of the *old* love and the substance of the *new*,—
The *then* of changeless sunny days—the *now* of shower and
    shine—
But Love forever smiling—as that old sweetheart of mine.

This ever-restful sense of *home*, though shouts ring in the
    hall.—
The easy chair—the old book-shelves and prints along the
    wall;
The rare *Habanas* in their box, or gaunt church-warden-stem
That often wags, above the jar, derisively at them.

As one who cons at evening o'er an album, all alone,
And muses on the faces of the friends that he has known,
So I turn the leaves of Fancy, till, in shadowy design,
I find the smiling features of an old sweetheart of mine.

The lamplight seems to glimmer with a flicker of surprise,
As I turn it low—to rest me of the dazzle in my eyes,
And light my pipe in silence, save a sigh that seems to yoke
Its fate with my tobacco and to vanish with the smoke.

'Tis a *fragrant* retrospection,—for the loving thoughts that
    start
Into being are like perfume from the blossom of the heart;
And to dream the old dreams over is a luxury divine—
When my truant fancies wander with that old sweetheart of
    mine.

Though I hear beneath my study, like a fluttering of wings,
The voices of my children and the mother as she sings—
I feel no twinge of conscience to deny me any theme
When Care has cast her anchor in the harbor of a dream—

In fact, to speak in earnest, I believe it adds a charm
To spice the good a trifle with a little dust of harm,—
For I find an extra flavor in Memory's mellow wine
That makes me drink the deeper to that old sweetheart of
    mine.

O Childhood-days enchanted! O the magic of the Spring!—
With all green boughs to blossom white, and all bluebirds to
    sing!
When all the air, to toss and quaff, made life a jubilee
And changed the children's song and laugh to shrieks of
    ecstasy.

With eyes half closed in clouds that ooze from lips that taste,
    as well,
The peppermint and cinnamon, I hear the old School bell,
And from "Recess" romp in again from "Blackman's" broken
    line,
To smile, behind my "lesson," at that old sweetheart of mine.

A face of lily beauty, with a form of airy grace,
Floats out of my tobacco as the Genii from the vase;
And I thrill beneath the glances of a pair of azure eyes
As glowing as the summer and as tender as the skies.

I can see the pink sunbonnet and the little checkered dress
She wore when first I kissed her and she answered the caress

With the written declaration that, "as surely as the vine
Grew 'round the stump," she loved me—that old sweetheart
    of mine.

Again I made her presents, in a really helpless way,—
The big "Rhode Island Greening"—I was hungry, too, that
    day!—
But I follow her from Spelling, with her hand behind
    her—so—
And I slip the apple in it—and the Teacher doesn't know!

I give my *treasures* to her—all,—my pencil—blue-and-red; —
And, if little girls played marbles, *mine* should all be *hers*, in-
    stead!
But *she* gave me her *photograph*, and printed "Ever Thine"
Across the back—in blue-and-red—that old sweetheart of
    mine!

And again I feel the pressure of her slender little hand,
As we used to talk together of the future we had planned,—
When I should be a poet, and with nothing else to do
But write the tender verses that she set the music to . . .

When we should live together in a cozy little cot
Hid in a nest of roses, with a fairy garden-spot,
Where the vines were ever fruited, and the weather ever fine,
And the birds were ever singing for that old sweetheart of
    mine.

When I should be her lover forever and a day,
And she my faithful sweetheart till the golden hair was gray;
And we should be so happy that when either's lips were dumb
They would not smile in Heaven till the other's kiss had come.

But, ah! my dream is broken by a step upon the stair,
And the door is softly opened, and—my wife is standing
    there:
Yet with eagerness and rapture all my visions I resign,—
To greet the *living* presence of that old sweetheart of mine.

SQUIRE HAWKINS'S STORY

I hain't no hand at tellin' tales,
Er spinnin' yarns, as the sailors say;
Someway o' 'nother, language fails
To slide fer me in the oily way
That *lawyers* has; and I wisht it would,
Fer I've got somepin' that I call good;
But bein' only a country squire,
I've learned to listen and admire,
Ruther preferrin' to be addressed
Than talk myse'f—but I'll do my best:—

Old Jeff Thompson—well, I'll say,
Was the clos'test man I ever saw!—
Rich as cream, but the porest pay,
And the meanest man to work fer—La!
I've knowed that man to work one "hand"—
Fer little er nothin', you understand—
From four o'clock in the morning light
Tel eight and nine o'clock at night,
And then find fault with his appetite!
He'd drive all over the neighborhood
To miss the place where a toll-gate stood,
And slip in town, by some old road
That no two men in the county knowed,
With a jag o' wood, and a sack o' wheat,
That wouldn't burn and you couldn't eat!

And the trades he'd make, 'll I jest declare,
Was enough to make a preacher swear!
And then he'd hitch, and hang about
Tel the lights in the toll-gate was blowed out,
And then the turnpike he'd turn in
And sneak his way back home ag'in!

Some folks hint, and I make no doubt,
That that's what wore his old wife out—
Toilin' away from day to day
And year to year, through heat and cold,
Uncomplainin'—the same old way
The martyrs died in the days of old;
And a-clingin', too, as the martyrs done,
To one fixed faith, and her *only* one,—
Little Patience, the sweetest child
That ever wept unrickonciled,
Er felt the pain and the ache and sting.
That only a mother's death can bring.

Patience Thompson!—I think that name
Must 'a' come from a power above,
Fer it seemed to fit her jest the same
As a *gaiter* would, er a fine kid glove!
And to see that girl, with all the care
Of the household on her—I de-clare
It was *oudacious*, the work she'd do,
And the thousand plans that she'd putt through;
And sing like a medder-lark all day long,
And drowned her cares in the joys o' song;
And *laugh* sometimes tel the farmer's "hand,"
Away fur off in the fields, would stand
A-listenin', with the plow half drawn,
Tel the coaxin' echoes called him on;
And the furries seemed, in his dreamy eyes,
Like foot-paths a-leadin' to Paradise,
As off through the hazy atmosphere
The call fer dinner reached his ear.

Now *love's* as cunnin' a little thing
As a hummin'-bird upon the wing,
And as liable to poke his nose
Jest where folks would least suppose,—
And more'n likely build his nest
Right in the heart you'd leave unguessed,
And live and thrive at your expense—

At least, that's *my* experience.
And old Jeff Thompson often thought,
In his se'fish way, that the quiet John
Was a stiddy chap, as a farm-hand *ought*
To always be,—fer the airliest dawn
Found John busy—and "*easy,*" too,
Whenever his *wages* would fall due!—
To sum him up with a final touch,
He *eat* so little and *worked* so much,
That old Jeff laughed to hisse'f and said,
"He makes *me* money and airns his bread!"

But John, fer all of his quietude,
Would sometimes drap a word er so
That none but *Patience* understood,
And none but her was *meant* to know!—
Maybe at meal-times John would say,
As the sugar-bowl come down his way,
"Thanky, no; *my* coffee's sweet
Enough fer *me!*" with sich conceit,
She'd know at once, without no doubt,
He meant because *she* poured it out;
And smile and blush, and all sich stuff,
And ast ef it was "*strong* enough?"
And git the answer, neat and trim,
"It *couldn't* be too 'strong' fer *him!*"

And so things went fer 'bout a year,
Tel John, at last, found pluck to go
And pour his tale in the old man's ear—
And ef it had been *hot lead*, I know
It couldn't 'a' raised a louder fuss,
Ner 'a' riled the old man's temper wuss!
He jest *lit* in, and cussed and swore,
And lunged and rared, and ripped and tore,
And told John jest to leave his door,
And not to darken it no more!
But Patience cried, with eyes all wet,
"Remember, John and don't ferget,

Whatever comes, I love you yet!"
But the old man thought, in his se'fish way,
"I'll see her married rich some day;
And *that*," thinks he, "is money fer *me*—
And my will's *law*, as it ought to be!"

So when, in the course of a month er so,
A *widower*, with a farm er two,
Comes to Jeff's, w'y, the folks, you know,
Had to *talk*—as the folks'll do:
It was the talk of the neighberhood—
Patience and *John*, and *their* affairs;—
And this old chap with a few gray hairs
Had "cut John out," it was understood.
And some folks reckoned "Patience, too,
Knowed what *she* was a-goin' to do—
It was *like* her—la! indeed!—
All *she* loved was *dollars* and *cents*—
Like old Jeff—and they saw no need
Fer *John* to pine at *her* negligence!"
But others said, in a *kinder* way,
They missed the songs she used to sing—
They missed the smiles that used to play
Over her face, and the laughin' ring
Of her glad voice—that *everything*
Of her *old* se'f seemed dead and gone,
And this was the ghost that they gazed on!

Tel finally it was noised about
There was a *weddin'* soon to be
Down at Jeff's; and the "cat was out"
Shore enough!—'Ll the *Jee-mum-nee*!
It *riled* me when John tole me so,—
Fer I *was* a *friend o'John's*, you know;
And his trimblin' voice jest broke in two—
As a feller's voice'll sometimes do.—
And I says, says I, "Ef I know my biz—
And I think I know what *jestice* is,—
I've read *some* law—and I'd advise

A man like you to wipe his eyes
And square his jaws and state *ag'in*,
Fer jestice is a-goin' to win!"
And it wasn't long tel his eyes had cleared
As blue as the skies, and the *sun* appeared
In the shape of a good old-fashioned smile
That I hadn't seen fer a long, long while.

So we talked on fer 'a' hour er more,
And sunned ourselves in the open door,—
Tel a hoss-and-buggy down the road
Come a-drivin' up, that I guess John *knowed*,—
Fer he winked and says, "I'll dessappear—
They'd smell a mice ef they saw *me* here!"
And he thumbed his nose at the old gray mare,
And hid hisse'f in the house somewhere.

Well.—The rig drove up: and I raised my head
As old Jeff hollered to me and said
That "him and his old friend there had come
To see ef the squire was at home."
. . . I told 'em "I was; and I *aimed* to be
At every chance of a weddin'-fee!"
And then I laughed—and they laughed, too,—
Fer that was the object they had in view.
"Would I be on hands at eight that night?"
They ast; and 's-I, "You're mighty right,
I'll be on hand!" And then I *bu'st*
Out a-laughin' my very wu'st,—
And so did they, as they wheeled away
And drove to'rds town in a cloud o' dust.
Then I shet the door, and me and John
Laughed and *laughed*, and jest *laughed* on,
Tel Mother drapped her specs, and *by
Jeewhillikers!* I thought she'd *die!*—
And she couldn't 'a' told, I'll bet my hat,
What on earth she was laughin' at!

But all o' the fun o' the tale hain't done! —
Fer a drizzlin' rain had jest begun,
And a-havin' 'bout four mile' to ride,
I jest concluded I'd better light
Out fer Jeff's and save my hide, —
Fer it was a-goin' to storm, that night!
So we went down to the barn, and John
Saddled my beast, and I got on;
And he told me somepin' to not ferget,
And when I left, he was *laughin'* yet.

And, 'proachin' on to my journey's end,
The great big draps o' the rain come down,
And the thunder growled in a way to lend
An awful look to the lowerin 'frown
The dull sky wore; and the lightnin' glanced
Tel my old mare jest *more'n* pranced,
And tossed her head, and bugged her eyes
To about four times their natchurl size,
As the big black lips of the clouds 'ud drap
Out some oath of a thunderclap,
And threaten on in an undertone
That chilled a feller clean to the bone!

But I struck shelter soon enough
To save myse'f. And the house was jammed
With the women-folks, and the weddin'-stuff: —
A great, long table, fairly *crammed*
With big pound-cakes—and chops and steaks—
And roasts and stews—and stumick-aches
Of every fashion, form, and size,
From twisters up to punkin-pies!
And candies, oranges, and figs,
And reezins,—all the "whilligigs"
And "jim-cracks" that the law allows
On sich occasions!—Bobs and bows
Of gigglin' girls, with corkscrew curls,
And fancy ribbons, reds and blues,
And "beau-ketchers" and "curliques"
To beat the world! And seven o'clock

Brought old Jeff;—and brought—*the groom*,—
With a sideboard-collar on, and stock
That choked him so, he hadn't room
To *swaller* in, er even sneeze,
Er clear his th'oat with any ease
Er comfort—and a good square cough
Would saw his Adam's apple off!

But as fer *Patience*—*My!* Oomh-*oomh!*—
I never saw her look so sweet!—
Her face was cream and roses, too;
And then them eyes o' heavenly blue
Jest made an angel all complete!
And when she split 'em up in smiles
And splintered 'em around the room,
And danced acrost and met the groom,
And *laughed out loud*—It kind o' spiles
My language when I come to that—
Fer, as she laid away his hat,
Thinks I, *"The papers hid inside*
Of that said hat must make a bride
A happy one fer all her life,
Er else a *wrecked* and *wretched wife!"*
And, someway, then, I thought of *John*,—
Then looked towards *Patience*. . . . She was *gone!*—
The door stood open, and the rain
Was dashin' in; and sharp and plain
Above the storm we heerd a cry—
A ringin', laughin', loud "Good-by!"
That died away, as fleet and fast
A hoss's hoofs went splashin' past!
And that was all. 'Twas done that quick! . . .
You've heerd o' fellers "lookin' sick"?
I wisht you'd seen *the groom* jest then—
I wisht you'd seen them two old men,
With starin' eyes that fairly *glared*
At one another, and the scared
And empty faces of the crowd,—
I wisht you could 'a' been allowed
To jest look on and see it all,—

And heerd the girls and women bawl
And wring their hands; and heerd old Jeff
A-cussin' as he swung hisse'f
Upon his hoss, who champed his bit
As though old Nick had holt of it:
And cheek by jowl the two old wrecks
Rode off as though they'd break their necks.

And as we all stood starin' out
Into the night, I felt the brush
Of some one's hand, and turned about,
And heerd a voice that whispered, "*Hush!*—
*They're waitin' in the kitchen, and
You're wanted. Don't you understand?*"
Well, ef my *memory* serves me now,
I think I winked.—Well, anyhow,
I left the crowd a-gawkin' there,
And jest slipped off around to where
The back door opened, and went in,
And turned and shet the door ag'in,
And maybe *locked* it—couldn't swear,—
A woman's arms around me makes
Me liable to make mistakes.—
I read a marriage license nex',
But as I didn't have my specs
I jest *inferred* it was all right,
And tied the knot so mortal-tight
That Patience and my old friend John
Was safe enough from that time on!

Well, now, I might go on and tell
How all the joke at last leaked out,
And how the youngsters raised the yell
And rode the happy groom about
Upon their shoulders; how the bride
Was kissed a hundred times beside
The one *I* give her,—tel she cried
And laughed untel she like to died!
I might to on and tell you all
About the supper—and the *ball.*—

You'd ought to see me twist my heel
Through jest one old Furginny reel
Afore you die! er tromp the strings
Of some old fiddle tel she sings
Some old cowtillion, don't you know,
That putts the devil in yer toe!

We kep' the dancin' up tel *four*
O'clock, I reckon—maybe more.—
We hardly heerd the thunders roar,
Er *thought* about the *storm* that blowed—
And them two fellers on the road!
Tel all at onc't we heerd the door
Bu'st open, and a voice that *swore*,—
And old Jeff Thompson tuck the floor.
He shuck hisse'f and looked around
Like some old dog about half-drowned—
His hat, I reckon, *weighted ten pound*
To say the least, and I'll say, *shore,*
His *overcoat weighed fifty* more—
The wettest man you ever saw,
To have so dry a son-in-law!

He sized it all; and Patience laid
Her hand in John's, and looked afraid,
And waited. And a stiller set
O'folks, I *know*, you never met
In any court room, where with dread
They wait to hear a verdick read.

The old man turned his eyes on me:
"And have you married 'em?" says he.
I nodded "Yes." "Well, that'll do,"
He says, "and now we're th'ough with *you*,—
You jest clear out, and I decide
And promise to be satisfied!"
He hadn't nothin' more to say.
I saw, of course, how matters lay,
And left. But as I rode away
I heerd the roosters crow fer day.

THE OLD GUITAR

Neglected now is the old guitar
And moldering into decay;
Fretted with many a rift and scar
  That the dull dust hides away,
While the spider spins a silver star
  In its silent lips to-day.

The keys hold only nerveless strings—
  The sinews of brave old airs
Are pulseless now; and the scarf that clings
  So closely here declares
A sad regret in its ravelings
  And the faded hue it wears.

But the old guitar, with a lenient grace,
  Has cherished a smile for me;
And its features hint of a fairer face
  That comes with a memory
Of a flower-and-perfume-haunted place
  And a moonlit balcony.

Music sweeter than words confess,
  Or the minstrel's powers invent,
Thrilled here once at the light caress
  Of the fairly hands that lent
This excuse for the kiss I press
  On the dear old instrument.

The rose of pearl with the jeweled stem
  Still blooms; and the tiny sets
In the circle all are here; the gem
  In the keys, and the silver frets;
But the dainty fingers that danced o'er them—
  Alas for the heart's regrets!—

Alas for the loosened strings to-day,
　　And the wounds of rift and scar
On a worn old heart, with its roundelay
　　Enthralled with a stronger bar
That Fate weaves on, through a dull decay
　　Like that of the old guitar!

THE SILENT VICTORS

Written for the Decoration Day ceremonies at Newcastle,
Indiana, in the centennial year, 1876.

I

Deep, tender, firm and true, the Nation's heart
  Throbs for her gallant heroes passed away,
Who in grim Battle's drama played their part,
  And slumber here to-day.—

Warm hearts that beat their lives out at the shrine
  Of Freedom, while our country held its breath
As brave battalions wheeled themselves in line
  And marched upon their death:

When Freedom's Flag, its natal wounds scarce healed,
  Was torn from peaceful winds and flung again
To shudder in the storm of battlefield—
  The elements of men,—

When every star that glittered was a mark
  For Treason's ball, and every rippling bar
Of red and white was sullied with the dark
  And purple stain of war:

When angry guns, like famished beasts of prey,
  Were howling o'er their gory feast of lives,
And sending dismal echoes far away
  To mothers, maids, and wives:—

The mother, kneeling in the empty night,
  With pleading hands uplifted for the son
Who, even as she prayed, had fought the fight—
  The victory had won:

The wife, with trembling hand that wrote to say
  The babe was waiting for the sire's caress—

[36]

The letter meeting that upon the way,—
  The babe was fatherless:

The maiden, with her lips, in fancy, pressed
  Against the brow once dewy with her breath,
Now lying numb, unknown, and uncaressed
  Save by the dews of death.

II

What meed of tribute can the poet pay
  The Soldier, but to trail the ivy-vine
Of idle rhyme above his grave to-day
  In epitaph design?—

Or wreathe with laurel-words the icy brows
  That ache no longer with a dream of fame,
But, pillowed lowly in the narrow house,
  Renowned beyond the name.

The dewy tear-drops of the night may fall,
  And tender morning with her shining hand
May brush them from the grasses green and tall
  That undulate the land.—

Yet song of Peace nor din of toil and thrift,
  Nor chanted honors, with the flowers we heap,
Can yield us hope the Hero's head to lift
  Out of its dreamless sleep:

The dear old Flag, whose faintest flutter flies
  A stirring echo through each patriot breast,
Can never coax to life the folded eyes
  That saw its wrongs redressed—

That watched it waver when the fight was hot,
  And blazed with newer courage to its aid,
Regardless of the shower of shell and shot
  Through which the charge was made;—

And when, at last, they saw it plume its wings,
  Like some proud bird in stormy element,
And soar untrammeled on its wanderings,
  They closed in death, content.

III

O Mother, you who miss the smiling face
  Of that dear boy who vanished from your sight,
And left you weeping o'er the vacant place
  He used to fill at night,—

Who left you dazed, bewildered, on a day
  That echoed wild huzzas, and roar of guns
That drowned the farewell words you tried to say
  To incoherent ones;—

Be glad and proud you had the life to give—
  Be comforted through all the years to come,—
Your country has a longer life to live,
  Your son a better home.

O Widow, weeping o'er the orphaned child,
  Who only lifts his questioning eyes to send
A keener pang to grief unreconciled,—
  Teach him to comprehend

He had a father brave enough to stand
  Before the fire of Treason's blazing gun,
That, dying, he might will the rich old land
  Of Freedom to his son.

And, Maiden, living on through lonely years
  In fealty to love's enduring ties,—
With strong faith gleaming through the tender tears
  That gather in your eyes,

Look up! and own, in gratefulness of prayer,
  Submission to the will of Heaven's High Host:—

I see your Angel-soldier pacing there,
    Expectant at his post. —

I see the rank and file of armies vast,
    That muster under one supreme control;
I hear the trumpet sound the signal-blast —
    The calling of the roll —

The grand divisions falling into line
    And forming, under voice of One alone
Who gives command, and joins with tongue divine
    The hymn that shakes the Throne.

IV

And thus, in tribute to the forms that rest
    In their last camping-ground, we strew the bloom
And fragrance of the flowers they loved the best,
    In silence o'er the tomb.

With reverent hands we twine the Hero's wreath
    And clasp it tenderly on stake or stone
That stands the sentinel for each beneath
    Whose glory is our own.

While in the violet that greets the sun,
    We see the azure eye of some lost boy;
And in the rose the ruddy cheek of one
    We kissed in childish joy, —

Recalling, haply, when he marched away,
    He laughed his loudest though his eyes were wet. —
The kiss he gave his mother's brow that day
    Is there and burning yet:

And through the storm of grief around her tossed,
    One ray of saddest comfort she may see, —

Four hundred thousand sons like hers were lost
　　To weeping Liberty.

　　　　　　·　·　·　·　·　·　·

But draw aside the drapery of gloom,
　　And let the sunshine chase the clouds away
And gild with brighter glory every tomb
　　We decorate to-day:

And in the holy silence reigning round,
　　While prayers of perfume bless the atmosphere,
Where loyal souls of love and faith are found,
　　Thank God that Peace is here!

And let each angry impulse that may start,
　　Be smothered out of evey loyal breast;
And, rocked within the cradle of the heart,
　　Let every sorrow rest.

HER BEAUTIFUL HANDS

O your hands—they are strangely fair!
Fair—for the jewels that sparkle there,—
Fair—for the witchery of the spell
That ivory keys alone can tell;
But when their delicate touches rest
Here in my own do I love them best,
As I clasp with eager, acquisitive spans
My glorious treasure of beautiful hands!

Marvelous—wonderful—beautiful hands!
They can coax roses to bloom in the strands
Of your brown tresses; and ribbons will twine,
Under mysterious touches of thine,
Into such knots as entangle the soul
And fetter the heart under such a control
As only the strength of my love understands—
My passionate love for your beautiful hands.

As I remember the first fair touch
Of those beautiful hands that I love so much,
I seem to thrill as I then was thrilled,
Kissing the glove that I found unfilled—
When I met your gaze, and the queenly bow,
As you said to me, laughingly, "Keep it now!" . . .
And dazed and alone in a dream I stand,
Kissing this ghost of your beautiful hand.

When first I loved, in the long ago,
And held your hand as I told you so—
Pressed and caressed it and gave it a kiss
And said "I could die for a hand like this!"
Little I dreamed love's fullness yet
Had to ripen when eyes were wet
And prayers were vain in their wild demands
For one warm touch of your beautiful hands.

. . . .

Beautiful Hands!—O Beautiful Hands!
Could you reach out of the alien lands
Where you are lingering, and give me, to-night,
Only a touch—were it ever so light—
My heart were soothed, and my weary brain
Would lull itself into rest again;
For there is no solace the world commands
Like the caress of your beautiful hands.

THE ROSE

It tossed its head at the wooing breeze;
   And the sun, like a bashful swain,
Beamed on it through the waving trees
   With a passion all in vain,—
For my rose laughed in a crimson glee,
And hid in the leaves in wait for me.

The honey-bee came there to sing
   His love through the languid hours,
And vaunt of his hives, as a proud old king
   Might boast of his palace-towers:
But my rose bowed in a mockery,
And hid in the leaves in wait for me.

The humming-bird, like a courtier gay,
   Dipped down with a dalliant song,
And twanted his wings through the roundelay
   Of love the whole day long:
Yet my rose turned from his minstrelsy
And hid in the leaves in wait for me.

The firefly came in the twilight dim
   My red, red rose to woo—
Till quenched was the flame of love in him,
   And the light of his lantern too,
As my rose wept with dewdrops three
And hid in the leaves in wait for me.

And I said: I will cull my own sweet rose—
   Some day I will claim as mine
The priceless worth of the flower that knows
   No change, but a bloom divine—
The bloom of a fadeless constancy
That hides in the leaves in wait for me!

But time passed by in a strange disguise,
    And I marked it not, but lay
In a lazy dream, with drowsy eyes,
    Till the summer slipped away,
And a chill wind sang in a minor key:
"Where is the rose that waits for thee?"

.   .   .   .

I dream to-day, o'er a purple stain
    Of bloom on a withered stalk,
Pelted down by the autumn rain
    In the dust of the garden-walk,
That an Angel-rose in the world to be
Will hide in the leaves in wait for me.

LEONAINIE

First printed in the Kokomo Dispatch with a trumped-up story linking it to Edgar Allan Poe. Riley had deliberately written it in Poe's style to prove his often repeated contention that none but established writers ever sold their poems —that an unknown poet had no chance. The story was readily accepted, and the poem was declared authentic by men of letters and literary critics.

Leonainie—Angels named her;
  And they took the light
Of the laughing stars and framed her
  In a smile of white;
    And they made her hair of gloomy
    Midnight, and her eyes of bloomy
    Moonshine, and they brought her to me
  In the solemn night.—

In a solemn night of summer,
  When my heart of gloom
Blossomed up to greet the comer
  Like a rose in bloom;
    All forebodings that distressed me
    I forgot as Joy caressed me—
    (*Lying* Joy! that caught and pressed me
  In the arms of doom!)

Only spake the little lisper
  In the Angel-tongue;
Yet I, listening, heard her whisper,—
  "Songs are only sung
    Here below that they may grieve you—
    Tales but told you to deceive you,—
    So must Leonainie leave you
  While her love is young."

Then God smiled and it was morning.
  Matchless and supreme
Heaven's glory seemed adorning
  Earth with its esteem:
    Every heart but mine seemed gifted
    With the voice of prayer, and lifted
    Where my Leonainie drifted
  From me like a dream.

FAME

Written in 1877 when Riley's own fame still lay in the future and when the poems he submitted to Eastern publishers were always rejected. His father liked "Fame" and thought it better than any of his previous poems.

I

Once, in a dream, I saw a man
  With haggard face and tangled hair,
  And eyes that nursed as wild a care
As gaunt Starvation ever can;
And in his hand he held a wand
  Whose magic touch gave life and thought
  Unto a form his fancy wrought
And robed with coloring so grand,
  It seemed the reflex of some child
  Of Heaven, fair and undefiled—
A face of purity and love—
To woo him into worlds above:
And as I gazed with dazzled eyes,
  A gleaming smile lit up his lips
  As his bright soul from its eclipse
Went flashing into Paradise.
Then tardy Fame came through the door
And found a picture—nothing more.

II

And once I saw a man, alone,
  In abject poverty, with hand
Uplifted o'er a block of stone
  That took a shape at his command
And smiled upon him, fair and good—
A perfect work of womanhood,
Save that the eyes might never weep,
Nor weary hands be crossed in sleep,
Nor hair that fell from crown to wrist,

[47]

Be brushed away, caressed and kissed.
And as in awe I gazed on her,
  I saw the sculptor's chisel fall—
    I saw him sink, without a moan,
    Sink lifeless at the feet of stone,
And lie there like a worshiper.
  Fame crossed the threshold of the hall,
  And found a statue—that was all.

III

And once I saw a man who drew
  A gloom about him like a cloak,
And wandered aimlessly. The few
  Who spoke of him at all but spoke
Disparagingly of a mind
The Fates had faultily designed:
Too indolent for modern times—
  Too fanciful, and full of whims—
For, talking to himself in rhymes,
  And scrawling never-heard-of hymns,
The idle life to which he clung
Was worthless as the songs he sung!
I saw him, in my vision, filled
  With rapture o'er a spray of bloom
  The wind threw in his lonely room;
And of the sweet perfume it spilled
He drank to drunkenness, and flung
His long hair back, and laughed and sung
And clapped his hands as children do
At fairy tales they listen to,
While from his flying quill there dripped
Such music on his manuscript
That he who listens to the words
May close his eyes and dream the birds
Are twittering on every hand
A language he can understand.
He journeyed on through life, unknown,
Without one friend to call his own;

He tired. No kindly hand to press
The cooling touch of tenderness
Upon his burning brow, nor lift
To his parched lips God's freest gift—
No sympathetic sob or sigh
Of trembling lips—no sorrowing eye
Looked out through tears to see him die.
And Fame her greenest laurels brought
To crown a head that heeded not.

And this is Fame! A thing, indeed,
That only comes when least the need:
The wisest minds of every age
The book of life from page to page
Have searched in vain; each lesson conned
Will promise it the page beyond—
Until the last, when dusk of night
Falls over it, and reason's light
Is smothered by that unknown friend
Who signs his *nom de plume*, The End.

"DREAM"

Because her eyes were far too deep
And holy for a laugh to leap
Across the brink where sorrow tried
To drown within the amber tide;
Because the looks, whose ripples kissed
The trembling lids through tender mist,
Were dazzled with a radiant gleam—
Because of this I called her "Dream."

Because the roses growing wild
About her features when she smiled
Were ever dewed with tears that fell
With tenderness ineffable;
Because her lips might spill a kiss
That, dripping in a world like this,
Would tincture death's myrrh-bitter stream
To sweetness—so I called her "Dream."

Because I could not understand
The magic touches of a hand
That seemed, beneath her strange control,
To smooth the plumage of the soul
And calm it, till, with folded wings,
It half forgot its flutterings,
And, nestled in her palm, did seem
To trill a song that called her "Dream."

Because I saw her, in a sleep
As dark and desolate and deep
And fleeting as the taunting night
That flings a vision of delight
To some lorn martyr as he lies
In slumber ere the day he dies—
Because she vanished like a gleam
Of glory, do I call her "Dream."

From THE FLYING ISLANDS
OF THE NIGHT

*A play about intrigue in fairy kingdoms, the only play Riley
ever wrote, was published in the* Indianapolis Saturday
Herald *in 1878. Here Princess Dwainie speaks to her
lover, Prince Amphine.*

                                                We talked
Of all the past, ah me! and all the friends
That now await my coming. And we talked
Of O so many things—so many things—
That I but blend them all with dreams of when,
With thy warm hand clasped close in this of mine
We cross the floating bridge that soon again
Will span the all-unfathomable gulfs
Of nether air betwixt this isle of strife
And my most glorious realm of changeless peace,
Where summer night reigns ever and the moon
Hangs ever ripe and lush with radiance
Above a land where roses float on wings
And fan their fragrance out so lavishly
That Heaven hath hint of it, and oft therefrom
Sends down to us across the odorous seas
Strange argosies of interchanging bud
And blossom, spice and balm.—Sweet—sweet
Beyond all art and wit of uttering.

THE TREE-TOAD

"'Scur'ous-Like," said the tree-toad,
  "I've twittered fer rain all day;
    And I got up soon,
    And hollered tel noon—
  But the sun, hit blazed away,
  Tel I jest clum down in a crawfish-hole,
  Weary at hart, and sick at soul!

"Dozed away fer an hour,
  And I tackled the thing ag'in:
    And I sung, and sung,
    Tel I knowed my lung
  Was jest about give in;
    And *then*, thinks I, ef hit don't rain *now*,
    They's nothin' in singin', anyhow!

"Onc't in a while some farmer
  Would come a-drivin' past;
    And he'd hear my cry,
    And stop and sigh—
  Tel I jest laid back, at last,
    And I hollered rain tel I thought my th'oat
    Would bust wide open at ever' note!

"But I *fetched* her!—O *I fetched* her!—
  'Cause a little while ago,
    As I kindo' set,
    With one eye shet,
  And a-singin' soft and low,
    A voice drapped down on my fevered brain,
    A-sayin',—'*Ef you'll jest hush I'll rain!*'"

THE LITTLE TOWN
O' TAILHOLT

You kin boast about yer cities, and their stiddy growth and
    size,
And brag about yer County-seats, and business enterprise,
And railroads, and factories, and all sich foolery—
But the little Town o' Tailholt is big enough fer me!

You kin harp about yer churches, with their steeples in the
    clouds,
And gas about yer graded streets, and blow about yer crowds;
You kin talk about yer "*the*aters," and all you've got to see—
But the little Town o' Tailholt is *show* enough fer me!

They hain't no *style* in our town—hit's little-like and small—
They hain't no "*churches*," nuther,—jes' the meetin'-house is
    all;
They's no sidewalks, to speak of—but the highway's allus free,
And the little Town o' Tailholt is wide enough fer me!

Some finds it discommodin'-like, I'm willing to admit
To hev but one post-office, and a womern keepin' hit,
And the drug-store, and shoe-shop, and grocery, all three—
But the little Town o' Tailholt is handy 'nough fer me!

You kin smile and turn yer nose up, and joke and hev yer fun,
And laugh and holler "Tail-holts is better holts'n none!"
Ef the city suits you better, w'y, hit's where you'd ort'o be—
But the little Town o' Tailholt's good enough fer me!

LOCKERBIE STREET

Such a dear little street it is, nestled away
From the noise of the city and heat of the day,
In cool shady coverts of whispering trees,
With their leaves lifted up to shake hands with the breeze
Which in all its wide wanderings never may meet
With a resting-place fairer than Lockerbie Street!

There is such a relief, from the clangor and din
Of the heart of the town, to go loitering in
Through the dim, narrow walks, with the sheltering shade
Of the trees waving over the long promenade,
And littering lightly the ways of our feet
With the gold of the sunshine of Lockerbie Street.

And the nights that come down the dark pathways of dusk,
With the stars in their tresses, and odors of musk
In their moon-woven raiments, bespangled with dews,
And looped up with lilies for lovers to use
In the songs that they sing to the tinkle and beat
Of their sweet serenadings through Lockerbie Street.

O my Lockerbie Street! You are fair to be seen—
Be it noon of the day, or the rare and serene
Afternoon of the night—you are one to my heart,
And I love you above all the phrases of art,
For no language could frame and no lips could repeat
My rhyme-haunted raptures of Lockerbie Street.

AT UTTER LOAF

I

An afternoon as ripe with heat
  As might the golden pippin be
  With mellowness if at my feet
It dropped now from the apple-tree
My hammock swings in lazily.

II

The boughs about me spread a shade
  That shields me from the sun, but weaves
  With breezy shuttles through the leaves
Blue rifts of skies, to gleam and fade
  Upon the eyes that only see
  Just of themselves, all drowsily.

III

Above me drifts the fallen skein
  Of some tired spider, looped and blown,
As fragile as a strand of rain,
  Across the air, and upward thrown
  By breaths of hay-fields newly mown—
So glimmering it is and fine,
I doubt these drowsy eyes of mine.

IV

Far-off and faint as voice pent
  In mines, and heard from underground,
Come murmurs as of discontent,
  And clamorings of sullen sound
The city sends me, as, I guess,
To vex me, though they do but bless
Me in my drowsy fastnesses.

V

I have no care. I only know
  My hammock hides and holds me here
  In lands of shade a prisoner:
While lazily the breezes blow
  Light leaves of sunshine over me,
And back and forth and to and fro
  I swing, enwrapped in some hushed glee,
  Smiling at all things drowsily.

THE USED-TO-BE

Beyond the purple, hazy trees
Of summer's utmost boundaries;
Beyond the sands—beyond the seas—
Beyond the range of eyes like these,
   And only in the reach of the
   Enraptured gaze of Memory,
   There lies a land, long lost to me,—
     The land of Used-to-be!

A land enchanted—such as swung
In golden seas when sirens clung
Along their dripping brinks, and sung
To Jason in that mystic tongue
   That dazed men with its melody—
   O such a land, with such a sea
   Kissing its shores eternally,
     Is the fair Used-to-be.

A land where music ever girds
The air with belts of singing-birds,
And sows all sounds with such sweet words,
That even in the low of herds
   A meaning lives so sweet to me,
   Lost laughter ripples limpidly
   From lips brimmed over with the glee
     Of rare old Used-to-be,

Lost laughter, and the whistled tunes
Of boyhood's mouth of crescent runes,
That rounded, through long afternoons,
To serenading plenilunes—
   When starlight fell so mistily
   That, peering up from bended knee,
   I dreamed 'twas bridal drapery
     Snowed over Used-to-be.

O land of love and dreamy thoughts,
And shining fields, and shady spots
Of coolest, greenest grassy plots,
Embossed with wild forget-me-nots! —
    And all ye blooms that longingly
    Lift your fair faces up to me
    Out of the past, I kiss in ye
        The lips of Used-to-be.

GRANDFATHER SQUEERS

"My grandfather Squeers," said The Raggedy Man,
As he solemnly lighted his pipe and began —

"The most indestructible man, for his years,
And the grandest on earth, was my grandfather Squeers!

"He said, when he rounded his three-score-and-ten,
'I've the hang of it now and can do it again!'

"He had frozen his heels so repeatedly, he
Could tell by them just what the weather would be;

"And would laugh and declare, 'while *the Almanac* would
Most falsely prognosticate, *he* never could!'

"Such a hale constitution had grandfather Squeers
That, though he'd used *'navy'* for sixty-odd years,

"He still chewed a dime's worth six days of the week,
While the seventh he passed with a chew in each cheek.

"Then my grandfather Squeers had a singular knack
Of sitting around on the small of his back.

"With his legs like a letter Y stretched o'er the grate
Wherein 'twas his custom to ex-pec-tor-ate.

"He was fond of tobacco in *manifold* ways,
And would sit on the door-step, of sunshiny days,

"And smoke leaf-tobacco he'd raised strictly for
The pipe he'd used all through the Mexican War."

And The Raggedy Man said, refilling the bowl
Of his *own* pipe and leisurely picking a coal

From the stove with his finger and thumb, "You can see
What a tee-nacious habit he's fastened on me!

"And my grandfather Squeers took a special delight
In pruning his corns every Saturday night

"With a horn-handled razor, whose edge he excused
By saying 'twas one that his grandfather used;

"And, though deeply etched in the haft of the same
Was the ever-euphonious Wostenholm's name,

"'Twas my grandfather's custom to boast of the blade
As 'a Seth Thomas razor—the best ever made!'

"No Old Settlers' Meeting, or Pioneers' Fair,
Was complete without grandfather Squeers in the chair,

"To lead off the program by telling folks how
'He used to shoot deer where the Court-house stands now'—

"How 'he felt, of a truth, to live over the past,
When the country was wild and unbroken and vast,

"'That the little log cabin was just plenty fine
For himself, his companion, and fambly of nine!—

"'When they didn't have even a pump, or a tin,
But drunk surface-water, year out and year in,

"'From the old-fashioned gourd that was sweeter, by odds,
Than the goblets of gold at the lips of the gods!'"

Then The Raggedy Man paused to plaintively say
It was clockin' along to'rds the close of the day—

And he'd *ought* to get back to his work on the lawn,—
Then dreamily blubbered his pipe and went on:

"His teeth were imperfect—my grandfather owned
That he couldn't eat oysters unless they were 'boned';

"And his eyes were so weak, and so feeble of sight,
He couldn't sleep with them unless, every night,

"He put on his spectacles—all he possessed,—
Three pairs—with his goggles on top of the rest.

"And my grandfather always, retiring at night,
Blew down the lamp-chimney to put out the light;

"Then he'd curl up on edge like a shaving, in bed,
And puff and smoke pipes in his sleep, it is said:

"And would snore oftentimes, as the legends relate,
Till his folks were wrought up to a terrible state,—

"Then he'd snort, and rear up, and roll over; and there
In the subsequent hush they could hear him chew air.

"And so glaringly bald was the top of his head
That many's the time he has musingly said,

"As his eyes journeyed o'er its reflex in the glass,—
'I must set out a few signs of *Keep Off the Grass*!'

"So remarkably deaf was my grandfather Squeers
That he had to wear lightning-rods over his ears

"To even hear thunder—and oftentimes then
He was forced to request it to thunder again."

THE PRAYER PERFECT

Dear Lord! kind Lord!
      Gracious Lord! I pray
Thou wilt look on all I love,
      Tenderly to-day!
Weed their hearts of weariness;
      Scatter every care
Down a wake of angel-wings
      Winnowing the air.

Bring unto the sorrowing
      All release from pain;
Let the lips of laughter
      Overflow again;
And with all the needy
      O divide, I pray,
This vast treasure of content
      That is mine to-day!

KISSING THE ROD

O heart of mine, we shouldn't
    Worry so!
What we've missed of calm we couldn't
    Have, you know!
What we've met of stormy pain,
And of sorrow's driving rain,
We can better meet again,
    If it blow!

We have erred in that dark hour
    We have known,
When our tears fell with the shower.
    All alone!—
Were not shine and shower blent
As the gracious Master meant?—
Let us temper our content
    With His own.

For, we know, not every morrow
    Can be sad;
So, forgetting all the sorrow
    We have had,
Let us fold away our fears,
And put by our foolish tears,
And through all the coming years
    Just be glad.

JACK THE GIANT-KILLER

Bad Boy's Version

Tell you a story—an' it's a fac':—
Wunst wuz a little boy, name wuz Jack,
An' he had sword an' buckle an' strap
Maked of gold, an' a "'visibul cap";
An' he killed Gi'nts 'at et whole cows—
Th' horns an' all—an' pigs an' sows!
But Jack, his golding sword wuz, oh!
So awful sharp 'at he could go
An' cut th' ole Gi'nts clean in two
'Fore 'ey knowed what he wuz goin' to do!
An' *one* ole Gi'nt, he had four
Heads, an' name wuz "Bumblebore"—
An' he wuz feared o' Jack—'cause he,
Jack, he killed six—five—ten—three,
An' all o' th' uther ole Gi'nts but him:
An' thay wuz a place Jack haf to swim
'Fore he could git t' ole "Bumblebore"—
Nen thay wuz "griffuns" at the door:
But Jack, he thist plunged in an' swum
Clean acrost; an' when he come
To th' uther side, he thist put on
His "'visibul cap," an' nen, dog-gone!
You couldn't see him at all!—An' so
He slewed the "griffuns"—*boff*, you know!
Nen wuz a horn hunged over his head,
High on th' wall, an' words 'at read,—
"Whoever kin this trumput blow
Shall cause the Gi'nt's overth'ow!"
An' Jack, he thist reached up an' blowed
The stuffin' out of it! an' th'owed
Th' castul gates wide open, an'
Nen tuk his gold sword in his han',
An' thist marched in t' ole "Bumblebore,"
An', 'fore he knowed, he put 'bout four
Heads on him—an' chopped 'em off, too!—
Wisht 'at *I'd* been Jack!—don't you?

THE NINE LITTLE GOBLINS

They all climbed up on a high board-fence—
  Nine little goblins, with green-glass eyes—
Nine little goblins that had no sense,
    And couldn't tell coppers from cold mince-pies;
      And they all climbed up on the fence, and sat—
      And I asked them what they were staring at.

And the first one said, as he scratched his head
  With a queer little arm that reached out of his ear
And rasped its claws in his hair so red—
    "This is what this little arm is fer!"
      And he scratched and stared, and the next one said,
      "How on earth do *you* scratch your head?"

And he laughed like the screech of a rusty hinge—
  Laughed and laughed till his face grew black;
And when he choked, with a final twinge
    Of his stifling laughter, he thumped his back
      With a fist that grew on the end of his tail
      Till the breath came back to his lips so pale.

And the third little goblin leered round at me—
  And there were no lids on his eyes at all,—
And he clucked one eye, and he says, says he,
    "What is the style of your socks this fall?"
      And he clapped his heels—and I sighed to see
      That he had hands where his feet should be.

Then a bald-faced goblin, gray and grim,
  Bowed his head, and I saw him slip
His eyebrows off, as I looked at him,
    And paste them over his upper lip;
      And then he moaned in remorseful pain—
      "Would—ah, would I'd me brows again!"

And then the whole of the goblin band
  Rocked on the fence-top to and fro,
And clung, in a long row, hand in hand,
    Singing the songs that they used to know—
      Singing the songs that their grandsires sung
      In the goo-goo days of the goblin-tongue.

And ever they kept their green-glass eyes
  Fixed on me with a stony stare—
Till my own grew glazed with a dread surmise,
    And my hat whooped up on my lifted hair,
      And I felt the heart in my breast snap to,
      As you've heard the lid of a snuff-box do.

And they sang: "You're asleep! There is no board-fence,
  And never a goblin with green-glass eyes!—
'Tis only a vision the mind invents
    After a supper of cold mince-pies,—
      And you're doomed to dream this way," they said,—
      "And you shan't wake up till you're clean plum dead!"

The Nine Little Goblins

THE ORCHARD LANDS
OF LONG AGO

The orchard lands of Long Ago!
O drowsy winds, awake, and blow
The snowy blossoms back to me,
And all the buds that used to be!
Blow back along the grassy ways
Of truant feet, and lift the haze
Of happy summer from the trees
That trail their tresses in the seas
Of grain that float and overflow
The orchard lands of Long Ago!

Blow back the melody that slips
In lazy laughter from the lips
That marvel much if any kiss
Is sweeter than the apple's is.
Blow back the twitter of the birds—
The lisp, the titter, and the words
Of merriment that found the shine
Of summer-time a glorious wine
That drenched the leaves that loved it so,
In orchard lands of Long Ago!

O memory! alight and sing
Where rosy-bellied pippins cling,
And golden russets glint and gleam,
As, in the old Arabian dream,
The fruits of that enchanted tree
The glad Aladdin robbed for me!
And, drowsy winds, awake and fan
My blood as when it overran
A heart ripe as the apples grow
In orchard lands of Long Ago!

THE DAYS GONE BY

O the days gone by! O the days gone by!
The apples in the orchard, and the pathway through the rye;
The chirrup of the robin, and the whistle of the quail
As he piped across the meadows sweet as any nightingale;
When the bloom was on the clover, and the blue was in the
    sky,
And my happy heart brimmed over, in the days gone by.

In the days gone by, when my naked feet were tripped
By the honeysuckle tangles where the water-lilies dipped,
And the ripples of the river lipped the moss along the brink
Where the placid-eyed and lazy-footed cattle came to drink,
And the tilting snipe stood fearless of the truant's wayward cry
And the splashing of the swimmer, in the days gone by.

O the days gone by! O the days gone by!
The music of the laughing lip, the luster of the eye;
The childish faith in fairies, and Aladdin's magic ring—
The simple, soul-reposing, glad belief in every thing,—
When life was like a story holding neither sob nor sigh,
In the golden olden glory of the days gone by.

THE CIRCUS-DAY PARADE

Oh, the Circus-Day Parade! How the bugles played and
    played!
And how the glossy horses tossed their flossy manes and
    neighed,
As the rattle and the rhyme of the tenor-drummer's time
Filled all the hungry hearts of us with melody sublime!

How the grand band-wagon shone with a splendor all its own,
And glittered with a glory that our dreams had never known!
And how the boys behind, high and low of every kind,
Marched in unconscious capture, with a rapture undefined!

How the horsemen, two and two, with their plumes of white
    and blue,
And crimson, gold and purple, nodding by at me and you,
Waved the banners that they bore, as the knights in days of
    yore,
Till our glad eyes gleamed and glistened like the spangles that
    they wore!

How the graceless-graceful stride of the elephant was eyed,
And the capers of the little horse that cantered at his side!
How the shambling camels, tame to the plaudits of their fame,
With listless eyes came silent, masticating as they came.

How the cages jolted past, with each wagon battened fast,
And the mystery within it only hinted of at last
From the little grated square in the rear, and nosing there
The snout of some strange animal that sniffed the outer air!

And, last of all, The Clown, making mirth for all the town,
With his lips curved ever upward and his eyebrows ever down,
And his chief attention paid to the little mule that played
A tattoo on the dashboard with his heels, in the Parade.

Oh! the Circus-Day Parade! How the bugles played and
    played!
And how the glossy horses tossed their flossy manes and
    neighed,
As the rattle and the rhyme of the tenor-drummer's time
Filled all the hungry hearts of us with melody sublime!

THE OLD SWIMMIN'-HOLE

This and the next nine poems (through "When the Frost Is on the Pumkin") appeared in the first book of Riley poems ever published, The Old Swimmin'-Hole and 'Leven Other Poems (1882). All were first published in the Indianapolis Journal, where they were signed, Benj. F. Johnson of Boone County. Accompanying editorial comment from Riley described the author, an uneducated, thoughtful old farmer who had been writing poetry since his youth. Riley's friends soon recognized the real hand behind the poems. All his life Riley enjoyed signing his letters with such whimsical names as James Popcorn Riley, Doc Marigold, Troubled Tom, Old E. Z. Mark, and "An Adjustable Lunatic." A favorite signature when he wrote to editors was James Hoosier Riley, the Whitcomb Poet.

Oh! the old swimmin'-hole! whare the crick so still and deep
Looked like a baby-river that was laying half asleep,
And the gurgle of the worter round the drift jest below
Sounded like the laugh of something we onc't ust to know
Before we could remember anything but the eyes
Of the angels lookin' out as we left Paradise;
But the merry days of youth is beyond our controle,
And it's hard to part ferever with the old swimmin'-hole.

Oh! the old swimmin'-hole! In the happy days of yore,
When I ust to lean above it on the old sickamore,
Oh! it showed me a face in its warm sunny tide
That gazed back at me so gay and glorified,
It made me love myself, as I leaped to caress
My shadder smilin' up at me with sich tenderness.
But them days is past and gone, and old Time's tuck his toll
From the old man come back to the old swimmin'-hole

Oh! the old swimmin'-hole! In the long, lazy days
When the humdrum of school made so many run-a-ways,
How plesant was the jurney down the old dusty lane,
Whare the tracks of our bare feet was all printed so plane
You could tell by the dent of the heel and the sole

They was lots o' fun on hands at the old swimmin'-hole.
But the lost joys is past! Let your tears in sorrow roll
Like the rain that ust to dapple up the old swimmin'-hole.

Thare the bullrushes growed, and the cattails so tall,
And the sunshine and shadder fell over it all;
And it mottled the worter with amber and gold
Tel the glad lilies rocked in the ripples that rolled;
And the snake-feeder's four gauzy wings fluttered by
Like the ghost of a daisy dropped out of the sky,
Or a wownded apple-blossom in the breeze's controle
As it cut acrost some orchurd to'rds the old swimmin'-hole.

Oh! the old swimmin'-hole! When I last saw the place,
The scenes was all changed, like the change in my face;
The bridge of the railroad now crosses the spot
Whare the old divin'-log lays sunk and fergot.
And I stray down the banks whare the trees ust to be—
But never again will theyr shade shelter me!
And I wish in my sorrow I could strip to the soul,
And dive off in my grave like the old swimmin'-hole.

THE CLOVER

Some sings of the lilly, and daisy, and rose,
And the pansies and pinks that the Summertime throws
In the green grassy lap of the medder that lays
Blinkin' up at the skyes through the sunshiny days;
But what is the lilly and all of the rest
Of the flowers, to a man with a hart in his brest
That was dipped brimmin' full of the honey and dew
Of the sweet clover-blossoms his babyhood knew?

I never set eyes on a clover-field now,
Er fool round a stable, er climb in the mow,
But my childhood comes back jest as clear and as plane
As the smell of the clover I'm sniffin' again;
And I wunder away in a barefooted dream,
Whare I tangle my toes in the blossoms that gleam
With the dew of the dawn of the morning of love
Ere it wept ore the graves that I'm weepin' above.

And so I love clover—it seems like a part
Of the sacerdest sorrows and joys of my hart;
And wherever it blossoms, oh, thare let me bow
And thank the good God as I'm thankin' Him now;
And I pray to Him still fer the stren'th when I die,
To go out in the clover and tell it good-bye,
And lovin'ly nestle my face in its bloom
While my soul slips away on a breth of purfume.

THOUGHTS FER THE DISCURAGED FARMER

The summer winds is sniffin' round the bloomin' locus' trees;
And the clover in the pastur is a big day fer the bees,
And they been a-swiggin' honey, above board and on the sly,
Tel they stutter in theyr buzzin' and stagger as they fly.
The flicker on the fence-rail 'pears to jest spit on his wings
And roll up his feathers, by the sassy way he sings;
And the hoss-fly is a-whettin'-up his forelegs fer biz,
And the off-mare is a-switchin' all of her tale they is.

You can hear the blackbirds jawin' as they foller up the
    plow—
Oh, theyr bound to git theyr brekfast, and theyr not a-carin'
    how;
So they quarrel in the furries, and they quarrel on the wing—
But theyr peaceabler in pot-pies than any other thing:
And it's when I git my shotgun drawed up in stiddy rest,
She's as full of tribbelation as a yeller-jacket's nest;
And a few shots before dinner, when the sun's a-shinin' right,
Seems to kindo'-sorto' sharpen up a feller's appetite!

They's been a heap o' rain, but the sun's out to-day,
And the clouds of the wet spell is all cleared away,
And the woods is all the greener, and the grass is greener still;
It may rain again to-morry, but I don't think it will.
Some says the crops is ruined, and the corn's drownded out,
And propha-sy the wheat will be a failure, without doubt;
But the kind Providence that has never failed us yet,
Will be on hands onc't more at the 'leventh hour, I bet!

Does the medder-lark complane, as he swims high and dry
Through the waves of the wind and the blue of the sky?
Does the quail set up and whissel in a disappinted way,
Er hand his head in silunce, and sorrow all the day?

Is the chipmuck's health a-failin'?—does he walk, er does he
    run?
Don't the buzzards ooze around up thare jest like they've allus
    done?
Is they anything the matter with the rooster's lungs er voice?
Ort a mortul be complanin' when dumb animals rejoice?

Then let us, one and all, be contentud with our lot;
The June is here this morning, and the sun is shining hot.
Oh! let us fill our harts up with the glory of the day,
And banish ev'ry doubt and care and sorrow fur away!
Whatever be our station, with Providence fer guide,
Sich fine circumstances ort to make us satisfied;
Fer the world is full of roses, and the roses full of dew,
And the dew is full of heavenly love that drips fer me and you.

WORTERMELON TIME

Old wortermelon time is a-comin' round ag'in,
  And they ain't no man a-livin' any tickleder'n me,
Fer the way I hanker after wortermelons is a sin—
  Which is the why and wharefore, as you can plainly see.

Oh! it's in the sandy soil wortermelons does the best,
  And it's thare they'll lay and waller in the sunshine and the
    dew
Tel they wear all the green streaks clean off of theyr breast;
  And you bet I ain't a-findin' any fault with them; air you?

They ain't no better thing in the vegetable line;
  And they don't need much 'tendin', as ev'ry farmer knows;
And when theyr ripe and ready fer to pluck from the vine,
  I want to say to you theyr the best fruit that grows.

It's some likes the yeller-core, and some likes the red,
  And it's some says "The Little Californy" is the best;
But the sweetest slice of all I ever wedged in my head,
  Is the old "Edingburg Mounting-sprout," of the West.

You don't want no punkins nigh your wortermelon vines—
  'Cause, some-way-another, they'll spile your melons,
    shore;—
I've seed 'em taste like punkins, from the core to the rines,
  Which may be a fact you have heerd of before.

But your melons that's raised right and 'tended to with care,
  You can walk around amongst 'em with a parent's pride and
    joy,
And thump 'em on the heads with as fatherly a air
  As ef each one of them was your little girl er boy.

I joy in my hart jest to hear that rippin' sound
  When you split one down the back and jolt the halves in
    two,

And the friends you love the best is gethered all around—
   And you says unto your sweethart, "Oh, here's the core fer
     you!"

And I like to slice 'em up in big pieces fer 'em all,
   Espeshally the children, and watch theyr high delight
As one by one the rines with theyr pink notches falls,
   And they holler fer some more, with unquenched appetite.

Boys takes to it natchurl, and I like to see 'em eat—
   A slice of wortermelon's like a frenchharp in theyr hands,
And when they "saw" it through theyr mouth sich music can't
    be beat—
   'Cause it's music both the sperit and the stummick under-
    stands.

Oh, they's more in wortermelons than the purty-colored meat,
   And the overflowin' sweetness of the worter squshed betwixt
The up'ard and the down'ard motions of a feller's teeth,
   And it's the taste of ripe old age and juicy childhood mixed.

Fer I never taste a melon but my thoughts flies away
   To the summer-time of youth; and again I see the dawn,
And the fadin' afternoon of the long summer day,
   And the dusk and dew a-fallin', and the night a-comin' on.

And thare's the corn around us, and the lispin' leaves and
    trees,
   And the stars a-peekin' down on us as still as silver mice,
And us boys in the wortermelons on our hands and knees,
   And the new-moon hangin' ore us like a yeller-cored slice.

Oh! it's wortermelon time is a-comin' round ag'in,
   And they ain't no man a-livin' any tickleder'n me,
Fer the way I hanker after wortermelons is a sin—
   Which is the why and wharefore, as you can plainly see.

MY FIDDLE

My fiddle?—Well, I kindo' keep her handy, don't you know!
Though I ain't so much inclined to tromp the strings and
    switch the bow
As I was before the timber of my elbows got so dry,
And my fingers was more limber-like and caperish and spry;
  Yit I can plonk and plunk and plink,
    And tune her up and play,
  And jest lean back and laugh and wink
    At ev'ry rainy day!

My playin' 's only middlin'—tunes I picked up when a boy—
The kindo'-sorto' fiddlin' that the folks call "cordaroy";
"The Old Fat Gal," and "Rye-straw," and "My Sailyor's on the
    Sea,"
Is the old cowtillions I "saw" when the ch'ice is left to me;
  And so I plunk and plonk and plink,
    And rosum-up my bow
  And play the tunes that makes you think
    The devil's in your toe!

I was allus a-romancin', do-less boy, to tell the truth,
A-fiddlin' and a-dancin', and a-wastin' of my youth,
And a-actin' and a-cuttin'-up all sorts o' silly pranks
That wasn't worth a button of anybody's thanks!
  But they tell me, when I used to plink
    And plonk and plunk and play,
  My music seemed to have the kink
    O' drivin' cares away!

That's how this here old fiddle's won my hart's indurin' love!
From the strings acrost her middle, to the schreechin' keys
    above—
From her "apern," over "bridge," and to the ribbon round her
    throat,

She's a wooin', cooin' pigeon, singin' "Love me" ev'ry note!
  And so I pat her neck, and plink
    Her strings with lovin' hands,—
  And, list'nin' clos't, I sometimes think
    She kindo' understands!

MY PHILOSOFY

I ain't, ner don't p'tend to be,
Much posted on philosofy;
But thare is times, when all alone,
I work out idees of my own.
And of these same thare is a few
I'd like to jest refer to you—
Pervidin' that you don't object
To listen clos't and rickollect.

I allus argy that a man
Who does about the best he can
Is plenty good enugh to suit
This lower mundane institute—
No matter ef his daily walk
Is subject fer his neghbor's talk,
And critic-minds of ev'ry whim
Jest all git up and go fer him!

I knowed a feller onc't that had
The yeller-janders mighty bad,—
And each and ev'ry friend he'd meet
Would stop and give him some receet
Fer cuorin' of 'em. But he'd say
He kindo' thought they'd go away
Without no medicin', and boast
That he'd git well without one doste.

He kep' a-yellerin' on—and they
Perdictin' that he'd die some day
Before he knowed it! Tuck his bed,
The feller did, and lost his head,
And wundered in his mind a spell—
Then rallied, and, at last, got well,
But ev'ry friend that said he'd die
Went back on him eternally!

It's natchurl enugh, I guess,
When some gits more and some gits less,
Fer them-uns on the slimmest side
To claim it ain't a fare divide;
And I've knowed some to lay and wait,
And git up soon, and set up late,
To ketch some feller they could hate
Fer goin' at a faster gait.

The signs is bad when folks commence
A-findin' fault with Providence,
And balkin' 'cause the earth don't shake
At ev'ry prancin' step they take.
No man is grate tel he can see
How less than little he would be
Ef stripped to self, and stark and bare
He hung his sign out anywhare.

My doctern is to lay aside
Contensions, and be satisfied:
Jest do you best, and praise er blame
That follers that, counts jest the same.
I've allus noticed grate success
Is mixed with troubles, more er less,
And it's the man who does the best
That gits more kicks than all the rest.

A SUMMER'S DAY

The Summer's put the idy in
  My head that I'm a boy ag'in;
  And all around's so bright and gay
  I want to put my team away,
  And jest git out whare I can lay
  And soak my hide full of the day!
But work is work, and must be done—
Yit, as I work, I have my fun,
Jest fancyin' these furries here
Is childhood's paths onc't more so dear:—
And so I walk through medder-lands,
  And country lanes, and swampy trails
Whare long bullrushes bresh my hands;
  And, tilted on the ridered rails
Of deadnin' fences, "Old Bob White"
Whissels his name in high delight,
And whirs away. I wunder still,
Whichever way a boy's feet will—
Whare trees has fell, with tangled tops
  Whare dead leaves shakes, I stop fer breth,
Heerin' the acorn as it drops—
  H'istin' my chin up still as deth,
And watchin' clos't , with upturned eyes,
The tree whare Mr. Squirrel tries
To hide hisse'f above the limb,
But lets his own tale tell on him.
I wunder on in deeper glooms—
  Git hungry, hearin' female cries
From old farmhouses, whare perfumes
  Of harvest dinners seems to rise
And ta'nt a feller, hart and brane,
With memories he can't explane.

I wunder through the underbresh,
  Whare pig-tracks, pintin' to'rds the crick,
Is picked and printed in the fresh
  Black bottom-lands, like wimmern pick
Theyr pie-crusts with a fork, some way,
When bakin' fer camp-meetin' day.

I wunder on and on and on,
Tel my gray hair and beard is gone,
And ev'ry wrinkle on my brow
Is rubbed clean out and shaddered now
With curls as brown and fare and fine
As tenderls of the wild grape-vine
That ust to climb the highest tree
To keep the ripest ones fer me.
I wunder still, and here I am
Wadin' the ford below the dam —
The worter chucklin' round my knee
  At hornet-welt and bramble-scratch,
And me a-slippin' 'crost to see
    Ef Tyner's plums is ripe, and size
  The old man's wortermelon-patch,
    With juicy mouth and drouthy eyes.
Then, after sich a day of mirth
And happiness as worlds is wurth —
  So tired that Heaven seems nigh about, —
The sweetest tiredness of earth
  Is to git home and flatten out —
So tired you can't lay flat enugh,
And sorto' wish that you could spred
Out like molasses on the bed,
And jest drip off the aidges in
The dreams that never comes ag'in.

ON THE DEATH OF
LITTLE MAHALA ASHCRAFT

"Little Haly! Little Haly!" cheeps the robin in the tree;
"Little Haly!" sighs the clover, "Little Haly!" moans the bee;
"Little Haly! Little Haly!" calls the killdeer at twilight;
And the katydids and crickets hollers "Haly!" all the night.

The sunflowers and the hollyhawks droops over the garden
    fence;
The old path down the garden walks still holds her footprints'
    dents;
And the well-sweep's swingin' bucket seems to wait fer her to
    come
And start it on its wortery errant down the old beegum.

The beehives all is quiet; and the little Jersey steer,
When any one comes nigh it, acts so lonesome-like and queer;
And the little Banty chickens kindo' cutters faint and low,
Like the hand that now was feedin' 'em was one they didn't
    know.

They's sorrow in the waivin' leaves of all the apple trees;
And sorrow in the harvest-sheaves, and sorrow in the breeze;
And sorrow in the twitter of the swallers 'round the shed;
And all the song her redbird sings is "Little Haly's dead!"

The medder 'pears to miss her, and the pathway through the
    grass,
Whare the dewdrops ust to kiss her little bare feet as she
    passed;
And the old pin in the gate-post seems to kindo'-sorto' doubt
That Haly's little sunburnt hands'll ever pull it out.

Did her father er her mother ever love her more'n me,
Er her sisters er her brother prize her love more tendurly?
I question—and what answer?—only tears, and tears alone,
And ev'ry neghbor's eyes is full o' tear-drops as my own.

"Little Haly! Little Haly!" cheeps the robin in the tree;
"Little Haly!" sighs the clover, "Little Haly!" moans the bee;
"Little Haly! Little Haly!" calls the killdeer at twilight,
And the katydids and crickets hollers "Haly!" all the night.

A HYMB OF FAITH

O, Thou that doth all things devise
   And fashon fer the best,
He'p us who sees with mortul eyes
   To overlook the rest.

They's times, of course, we grope in doubt,
   And in afflictions sore;
So knock the louder, Lord, without,
   And we'll unlock the door.

Make us to feel, when times looks bad
   And tears in pitty melts,
Thou wast the only he'p we had
   When they was nothin' else.

Death comes alike to ev'ry man
   That ever was borned on earth;
Then let us do the best we can
   To live fer all life's wurth.

Ef storms and tempusts dred to see
   Makes black the heavens ore,
They done the same in Galilee
   Two thousand years before.

But after all, the golden sun
   Poured out its floods on them
That watched and waited fer the One
   Then borned in Bethlyham.

Also, the star of holy writ
   Made noonday of the night,
Whilse other stars that looked at it
   Was envious with delight.

The sages then in wurship bowed,
    From ev'ry clime so fare;
O, sinner, think of that glad crowd
    That congergated thare!

They was content to fall in ranks
    With One that knowed the way
From good old Jurden's stormy banks
    Clean up to Jedgmunt Day.

No matter, then, how all is mixed
    In our near-sighted eyes,
All things is fer the best, and fixed
    Out straight in Paradise.

Then take things as God sends 'em here,
    And, ef we live er die,
Be more and more contenteder,
    Without a-astin' why.

O, Thou that doth all things devise
    And fashon fer the best,
He'p us who sees with mortul eyes
    To overlook the rest.

WHEN THE FROST
IS ON THE PUNKIN

When the frost is on the punkin and the fodder's in the shock,
And you hear the kyouck and gobble of the struttin' turkey-
    cock,
And the clackin' of the guineys, and the cluckin' of the hens,
And the rooster's hallylooer as he tiptoes on the fence;
O, it's then's the times a feller is a-feelin' at his best,
With the risin' sun to greet him from a night of peaceful rest,
As he leaves the house, bareheaded, and goes out to feed the
    stock,
When the frost is on the punkin and the fodder's in the shock.

They's something kindo' harty-like about the atmusfere
When the heat of summer's over and the coolin' fall is here—
Of course we miss the flowers, and the blossums on the trees,
And the mumble of the hummin'-birds and buzzin' of the
    bees;
But the air's so appetizin'; and the landscape through the haze
Of a crisp and sunny morning of the airly autumn days
Is a pictur' that no painter has the colorin' to mock—
When the frost is on the punkin and the fodder's in the shock.

The husky, rusty russel of the tossels of the corn,
And the raspin' of the tangled leaves, as golden as the morn;
The stubble in the furries—kindo' lonesome-like, but still
A-preachin' sermons to us of the barns they growed to fill;
The strawstack in the medder, and the reaper in the shed;
The hosses in theyr stalls below—the clover overhead!—
O, it sets my hart a-clickin' like the tickin' of a clock,
When the frost is on the punkin and the fodder's in the shock!

Then your apples all is gethered, and the ones a feller keeps
Is poured around the celler-floor in red and yeller heaps;
And your cider-makin' 's over, and your wimmern-folks is
    through
With their mince and apple-butter, and theyr souse and saus-
    sage, too! . . .
I don't know how to tell it—but ef sich a thing could be
As the Angels wantin' boardin', and they'd call around on
    me —
I'd want to 'commodate 'em—all the whole-indurin' flock—
When the frost is on the punkin and the fodder's in the shock!

AN AUTUMNAL TONIC

What mystery is it? The morning as rare
  As the Indian Summer may bring!
A tang in the frost and a spice in the air
  That no city poet can sing!
The crimson and amber and gold of the leaves,
  As they loosen and flutter and fall
In the path of the park, as it rustlingly weaves
Its way through the maples and under the eaves
  Of the sparrows that chatter and call.

What hint of delight is it tingles me through?—
  What vague, indefinable joy?
What yearning for something divine that I knew
  When a wayward and wood-roving boy?
Ah-ha! and Oho! but I have it, I say—
  Oh, the mystery brightens at last,—
'Tis the longing and zest of the far, far away,
For a bountiful, old-fashioned dinner to-day,
  With the hale harvest-hands of the past.

"THE PREACHER'S BOY"

I rickollect the little tad, back, years and years ago—
"The Preacher's Boy" that every one despised and hated so!
A meek-faced little feller, with white eyes and foxy hair,
And a look like he expected ser'ous trouble everywhere:
A sort o' fixed expression of suspicion in his glance;
His bare feet always scratched with briers; and green stains on
    his pants;
Molasses-marks along his sleeves; his cap-rim turned
    behind—
And so it is "The Preacher's Boy" is brought again to mind!

My fancy even brings the sly marauder back so plain,
I see him jump our garden-fence and slip off down the lane;
And I seem to holler at him and git back the old reply:
"Oh, no: your peaches is too green fer such a worm as I!"
Fer he scorned his father's phrases—every holy one he had—
"As good a man," folks put it, "as that boy of his was bad!"
And again from their old buggy-shed, I hear the "rod un-
    spared"—
Of course that never "spoiled the child" for which nobody
    cared!

If any neighber ever found his gate without a latch,
Or rines around the edges of his watermelon-patch;
His pasture-bars left open; or his pump-spout chocked with
    clay,
He'd swear 'twas "that infernal Preacher's Boy," right away!
When strings was stretched acrost the street at night, and
    some one got
An everlastin' tumble, and his nose broke, like as not,
And laid it on "The Preacher's Boy"—no powers, low ner
    high,
Could ever quite substantiate that boy's alibi!

And did *nobody* like the boy?—Well, all the *pets* in town
Would eat out of his fingers; and canaries would come down
And leave their swingin' perches and their fish-bone jist to
    pick
The little warty knuckles that the dogs would leap to lick.—
No little snarlin', snappin' fiste but what would leave his bone
To foller, ef *he* whistled, in that tantalizin' tone
That made a goods-box whittler blasphemeusly protest
"He couldn't tell, 'twixt dog and boy, which one was ornriest!"

'Twas such a little cur as this, onc't, when the crowd was thick
Along the streets, a drunken corner-loafer tried to kick,
When a sudden foot behind him tripped him up, and falling
    so
He "marked his man," and jerked his gun—drawed up and let
    'er go!
And the crowd swarmed round the victim—holding close
    against his breast
The little dog unharmed, in arms that still, as they caressed,
Grew rigid in their last embrace, as with a smile of joy
He recognized the dog was saved. So died "The Preacher's
    Boy"!

When it appeared, before the Squire, that fatal pistol-ball
Was fired at "a dangerous beast," and not the boy at all,
And the facts set forth established,—it was like-befittin' then
To order out a possy of the "city councilmen"
To kill *the dog*! But, strange to tell, they searched the country
    round,
And never hide-ner-hair of that "said" dog was ever found!
And, somehow, *then* I sort o' thought—and half-way think,
    to-day—
The spirit of "The Preacher's Boy" had whistled him away.

A SUDDEN SHOWER

Barefooted boys scud up the street
  Or skurry under sheltering sheds;
And schoolgirl faces, pale and sweet,
  Gleam from the shawls about their heads.

Doors bang; and mother-voices call
  From alien homes; and rusty gates
Are slammed; and high above it all,
  The thunder grim reverberates.

And then, abrupt,—the rain! the rain!
  The earth lies gasping; and the eyes
Behind the streaming window-pane
  Smile at the trouble of the skies.

The highway smokes; sharp echoes ring;
  The cattle bawl and cow-bells clank;
And into town comes galloping
  The farmer's horse, with steaming flank.

The swallow dips beneath the eaves
  And flirts his plumes and folds his wings;
And under the Catawba leaves
  The caterpillar curls and clings.

The bumblebee is pelted down
  The wet stem of the hollyhock;
And sullenly, in spattered brown,
  The cricket leaps the garden-walk.

Within, the baby claps his hands
  And crows with rapture strange and vague;
Without, beneath the rose-bush stands
  A dripping rooster on one leg.

THE MAN IN THE MOON

Said The Raggedy Man, on a hot afternoon:
   My!
       Sakes!
           What a lot o' mistakes
Some little folks makes on The Man in the Moon!
But people that's be'n up to *see* him, like *me*,
And calls on him frequent and intimuttly,
Might drop a few facts that would interest you
   Clean!
       Through!—
           If you wanted 'em to—
Some *actual* facts that might interest you!

O The Man in the Moon has a crick in his back;
   Whee!
       Whimm!
           Ain't you sorry for him?
And a mole on his nose that is purple and black;
And his eyes are so weak that they water and run
If he dares to *dream* even he looks at the sun,—
So he jes' dreams of stars, as the doctors advise—
   My!
       Eyes!
           But isn't he wise—
To jes' dream of stars, as the doctors advise?

And The Man in the Moon has a boil on his ear—
   Whee!
       Whing!
           What a singular thing!
I know! but these facts are authentic, my dear,—
There's a boil on his ear; and a corn on his chin—
He calls it a dimple—but dimples stick in—
Yet it might be a dimple turned over, you know!
   Whang!

Ho!
     Why, certainly so!—
It might be a dimple turned over, you know!

And The Man in the Moon has a rheumatic knee—
    Gee!
       Whizz!
         What a pity that is!
And his toes have worked round where his heels ought to
    be.—
So whenever he wants to go North he goes *South*,
And comes back with porridge-crumbs all round his mouth,
And he brushes them off with a Japanese fan,
    Whing!
       Whann!
         What a marvelous man!
What a very remarkably marvelous man!

And The Man in the Moon, sighed The Raggedy Man,
    Gits!
      So!
         Sullonesome, you know,—
Up there by hisse'f sence creation began!—
That when *I* call on him and then come away,
He grabs me and holds me and begs me to stay,—
Till—*Well*! if it wasn't fer *Jimmy-cum-jim*,
    Dadd!
      Limb!
         I'd go pardners with him—
Jes jump my job here and be pardners with *him*!

THE ALL-GOLDEN

I

Through every happy line I sing
I feel the tonic of the Spring.
The day is like an old-time face
That gleams across some grassy place—
An old-time face—an old-time chum
Who rises from the grave to come
And lure me back along the ways
Of time's all-golden yesterdays.
Sweet day! to thus remind me of
The truant boy I used to love—
To set, once more, his finger-tips
Against the blossom of his lips,
And pipe for me the signal known
By none but him and me alone!

II

I see, across the schoolroom floor,
The shadow of the open door,
And dancing dust and sunshine blent
Slanting the way the morning went,
And beckoning my thoughts afar
Where reeds and running waters are;
Where amber-colored bayous glass
The half-drown'd weeds and wisps of grass,
Where sprawling frogs, in loveless key,
Sing on and on incessantly.
Against the green wood's dim expanse
The cattail tilts its tufted lance,
While on its tip—one might declare
The white "snake-feeder" blossomed there!

I catch my breath, as children do
In woodland swings when life is new,
And all the blood is warm as wine
And tingles with a tang divine.
My soul soars up the atmosphere
And sings aloud where God can hear,
And all my being leans intent
To mark His smiling wonderment.
O gracious dream, and gracious time,
And gracious theme, and gracious rhyme—
When buds of Spring begin to blow
In blossoms that we used to know
And lure us back along the ways
Of time's all-golden yesterdays!

NOTHIN' TO SAY

Nothin' to say, my daughter! Nothin' at all to say!
Gyrls that's in love, I've noticed, giner'ly has their way!
Yer mother did, afore you, when her folks objected to me—
Yit here I am and here you air! and yer mother—where is
    she?

You look lots like yer mother: purty much same in size;
And about the same complected; and favor about the eyes:
Like her, too, about livin' here, because *she* couldn't stay;
It'll most seem like you was dead like her!—but I hain't got
    nothin' to say!

She left you her little Bible—writ yer name acrost the page—
And left her ear-bobs fer you, ef ever you come of age;
I've alluz kep' 'em and gyuarded 'em, but ef yer goin' away—
Nothin' to say, my daughter! Nothin' at all to say!

You don't rickollect her, I reckon? No: you wasn't a year old
    then!
And now yer—how old *air* you? W'y, child, not *"twenty"*!
    When?
And yer nex' birthday's in Aprile? and you want to git married
    that day?
I wisht yer mother was livin'!—but I hain't got nothin' to say!

Twenty year! and as good a gyrl as parent ever found!
There's a straw ketched on to yer dress there—I'll bresh it
    off—turn round.
(Her mother was jes' twenty when us two run away.)
Nothin' to say, my daughter! Nothin' at all to say!

WET-WEATHER TALK

It hain't no use to grumble and complane;
   It's jest as cheap and easy to rejoice.—
When God sorts out the weather and sends rain,
W'y, rain's my choice.

Men ginerly, to all intents—
   Although they're apt to grumble some—
Puts most theyr trust in Providence,
   And takes things as they come—
      That is, the commonality
      Of men that's lived as long as me
      Has watched the world enugh to learn
      They're not the boss of this concern.

With *some*, of course, it's different—
   I've saw *young* men that knowed it all,
And didn't like the way things went
   On this terrestchul ball;—
      But all the same, the rain, some way,
      Rained jest as hard on picnic day;
      Er, when they railly *wanted* it,
      It maybe wouldn't rain a bit!

In this existunce, dry and wet
   Will overtake the best of men—
Some little skift o' clouds'll shet
   The sun off now and then.—
And mayby, whilse you're wundern who
You've fool-like lent your umbrella to,
And *want* it—out'll pop the sun,
And you'll be glad you hain't got none!

It aggervates the farmers, too—
　　They's too much wet, er too much sun,
Er work, er waitin' round to do
　　Before the plowin' 's done:
　　　　And mayby, like as not, the wheat,
　　　　Jest as it's lookin' hard to beat,
　　　　Will ketch the storm—and jest about
　　　　The time the corn's a-jintin' out.

These-here *cy-clones* a-foolin' round—
　　And back'ard crops!—and wind and rain!—
And yit the corn that's wallerd down
　　May elbow up again!—
　　　　They hain't no sense, as I can see,
　　　　Fer mortuls, sich as us, to be
　　　　A-faultin' Natchur's wise intents,
　　　　And lockin' horns with Providence!

It hain't no use to grumble and complane;
　　It's jest as cheap and easy to rejoice.—
When God sorts out the weather and sends rain,
　　W'y, rain's my choice.

THE PIXY PEOPLE

It was just a very
  Merry fairy dream!—
All the woods were airy
  With the gloom and gleam;
Crickets in the clover
  Clattered clear and strong,
And the bees droned over
  Their old honey-song!

In the mossy passes,
  Saucy grasshoppers
Leaped about the grasses
  And the thistle-burs;
And the whispered chuckle
  Of the katydid
Shook the honeysuckle-
  Blossoms where he hid.

Through the breezy mazes
  Of the lazy June,
Drowsy with the hazes
  Of the dreamy noon,
Little Pixy people
  Winged above the walk,
Pouring from the steeple
  Of a mullein-stalk.

One—a gallant fellow—
  Evidently King,—
Wore a plume of yellow
  In a jeweled ring
On a pansy bonnet,
  Gold and white and blue,
With the dew still on it,
  And the fragrance, too.

One—a dainty lady,—
  Evidently Queen—
Wore a gown of shady
  Moonshine and green,
With a lace of gleaming
  Starlight that sent
All the dewdrops dreaming
  Everywhere she went.

One wore a waistcoat
  Of rose-leaves, out and in;
And one wore a faced-coat
  Of tiger-lily-skin;
And one wore a neat coat
  Of palest galingale;
And one a tiny street-coat,
  And one a swallow-tail.

And Ho! sang the King of them,
  And Hey! sang the Queen;
And round and round the ring of them
  Went dancing o'er the green;
And Hey! sang the Queen of them,
  And Ho! sang the King—
And all that I had seen of them
  —Wasn't anything!

It was just a very
  Merry fairy dream!—
All the woods were airy
  With the gloom and gleam;
Crickets in the clover
  Clattered clear and strong,
And the bees droned over
  Their old honey-song!

OUT TO OLD AUNT MARY'S

The first version, a letter written in 1893 to Riley's brother John, who was then living in the West, was six stanzas long. Riley later added another four stanzas. This was one of his favorite poems, and he often used it on the lecture platform. In 1904 the final version, with ten more new stanzas, was published.

Wasn't it pleasant, O brother mine,
In those old days of the lost sunshine
  Of youth—when the Saturday's chores were through,
  And the "Sunday's wood" in the kitchen, too,
  And we went visiting, "me and you,"
    Out to Old Aunt Mary's?—

"Me and you"—And the morning fair,
With the dewdrops twinkling everywhere;
  The scent of the cherry-blossoms blown
  After us, in the roadway lone,
  Our capering shadows onward thrown—
    Out to Old Aunt Mary's.

It all comes back so clear to-day!
Though I am as bald as you are gray,—
  Out by the barn-lot and down the lane
  We patter along in the dust again,
  As light as the tips of the drops of the rain,
    Out to Old Aunt Mary's.

The last few houses of the town;
Then on, up the high creek-bluffs and down;
  Past the squat toll-gate, with its well-sweep pole;
  The bridge, and "the old 'babtizin'-hole,'"
  Loitering, awed, o'er pool and shoal,
    Out to Old Aunt Mary's.

We cross the pasture, and through the wood,
Where the old gray snag of the poplar stood,
  Where the hammering "red-heads" hopped awry,
  And the buzzard "raised" in the "clearing"-sky
  And lolled and circled, as we went by
    Out to Old Aunt Mary's.

Or, stayed by the glint of the redbird's wings,
Or the glitter of song that the bluebird sings,
  All hushed we feign to strike strange trails,
  As the "big braves" do in the Indian tales,
  Till again our real quest lags and fails—
    Out to Old Aunt Mary's.—

And the woodland echoes with yells of mirth
That make old war-whoops of minor worth! . . .
  Where such heroes of war as we?—
  With bows and arrows of fantasy,
  Chasing each other from tree to tree
    Out to Old Aunt Mary's!

And then in the dust of the road again;
And the teams we met, and the countrymen;
  And the long highway, with sunshine spread
  As thick as butter on country bread,
  Our cares behind, and our hearts ahead
    Out to Old Aunt Mary's.—

For only, now, at the road's next bend
To the right we could make out the gable-end
  Of the fine old Huston homestead—not
  Half a mile from the sacred spot
  Where dwelt our Saint in her simple cot—
    Out to Old Aunt Mary's.

Why, I see her now in the open door
Where the little gourds grew up the sides and o'er
  The clapboard roof!—And her face—ah, me!
  Wasn't it good for a boy to see—

And wasn't it good for a boy to be
    Out to Old Aunt Mary's?—

The jelly—the jam and the marmalade,
And the cherry and quince "preserves" she made!
  And the sweet-sour pickles of peach and pear,
  With cinnamon in 'em and all things rare!—
  And the more we ate was the more to spare,
    Out to Old Aunt Mary's!

Ah, was there, ever, so kind a face
And gentle as hers, or such a grace
  Of welcoming, as she cut the cake
  Or the juicy pies that she joyed to make
  Just for the visiting children's sake—
    Out to Old Aunt Mary's!

The honey, too, in its amber comb
One only finds in an old farm-home;
  And the coffee, fragrant and sweet, and ho!
  So hot that we gloried to drink it so,
  With spangles of tears in our eyes, you know—
    Out to Old Aunt Mary's.

And the romps we took, in our glad unrest!—
Was it the lawn that we loved the best,
  With its swooping swing in the locust trees,
  Or was it the grove, with its leafy breeze,
  Or the dim haymow, with its fragrancies—
    Out to Old Aunt Mary's.

Far fields, bottom-lands, creek-banks—all,
We ranged at will.—Where the waterfall
  Laughed all day as it slowly poured
  Over the dam by the old mill-ford,
  While the tail-race writhed, and the mill-wheel roared—
    Out to Old Aunt Mary's.

But home, with Aunty in nearer call,
That was the best place, after all!—
   The talks on the back porch, in the low
   Slanting sun and the evening glow,
   With the voice of counsel that touched us so,
     Out to Old Aunt Mary's.

And then, in the garden—near the side
Where the beehives were and the path was wide,—
   The apple-house—like a fairy cell—
   With the little square door we knew so well,
   And the wealth inside but our tongues could tell—
     Out to Old Aunt Mary's.

And the old spring-house, in the cool green gloom
Of the willow trees,—and the cooler room
   Where the swinging shelves and the crocks were kept,
   Where the cream in a golden languor slept,
   While the waters gurgled and laughed and wept—
     Out to Old Aunt Mary's.

And as many a time have you and I—
Barefoot boys in the days gone by—
   Knelt, and in tremulous ecstasies
   Dipped our lips into sweets like these,—
   Memory now is on her knees
     Out to Old Aunt Mary's.—

For, O my brother so far away,
This is to tell you—she waits *to-day*
   To welcome us:—Aunt Mary fell
   Asleep this morning, whispering, "Tell
   The boys to come." . . . And all is well
     Out to Old Aunt Mary's.

AWAY

I can not say, and I will not say
That he is dead. — He is just away!

With a cheery smile, and a wave of the hand,
He has wandered into an unknown land,

And left us dreaming how very fair
It needs must be, since he lingers there.

And you — O you, who the wildest yearn
For the old-time step and the glad return, —

Think of him faring on, as dear
In the love of There as the love of Here;

And loyal still, as he gave the blows
Of his warrior-strength to his country's foes. —

Mild and gentle, as he was brave, —
When the sweetest love of his life he gave

To simple things: — Where the violets grew
Blue as the eyes they were likened to,

The touches of his hands have strayed
As reverently as his lips have prayed:

When the little brown thrush that harshly chirred
Was dear to him as the mocking-bird;

And he pitied as much as a man in pain
A writhing honey-bee wet with rain. —

Think of him still as the same, I say:
He is not dead — he is just away!

ON THE BANKS O' DEER CRICK

*Deer Creek is near Delphi in Carroll County, Indiana.
Riley first visited the area in 1883 to give a lecture on
"Characteristics of Western Humor." He made frequent return visits. "If there was no opportunity to go to Delphi," he
said, "I made one. It was a refuge from the sweltering heat
of the city." Near Delphi he met a farmer whose idea of
Eden was Deer Creek—"On the banks o' Deer Crick's grand
enough fer me."*

On the banks o' Deer Crick! there's the place fer me!—
Worter slidin' past ye jes' as clair as it kin be:—
See yer shadder in it, and the shadder o' the sky,
And the shadder o' the buzzard as he goes a-lazin' by;
Shadder o' the pizen-vines, and shadder o' the trees—
And I purt' nigh said the shadder o' the sunshine and the
    breeze!
Well—I never seen the ocean ner I never seen the sea:—
On the banks o' Deer Crick's grand enough fer me!

On the banks o' Deer Crick—mil'd er two from town—
'Long up where the mill-race comes a-loafin' down,—
Like to git up in there—'mongst the sycamores—
And watch the worter at the dam, a-frothin' as she pours:
Crawl out on some old log, with my hook and line,
Where the fish is jes' so thick you kin see 'em shine
As they flicker round yer bait, *coaxin'* you to jerk,
Tel yer tired ketchin' of 'em, mighty nigh, as *work*!

On the banks o' Deer Crick!—Allus my delight
Jes' to be around there—take it day er night!—
Watch the snipes and killdees foolin' half the day—
Er these-'ere little worter-bugs skootin' ever' way!—
Snake-feeders glancin' round, er dartin' out o' sight;
And dewfall, and bullfrogs, and lightnin'-bugs at night—
Stars up through the tree-tops—er in the crick below,—
And smell o' mussrat through the dark clean from the old
    by-o!

Er take a tromp, some Sund'y, say, 'way up to "Johnson's
    Hole,"
And find where he's had a fire, and hid his fishin'-pole:
Have yer "dog-leg" with ye, and yer pipe and "cut-and-dry"—
Pocketful o' corn-bread, and slug er two o' rye. . . .
Soak yer hide in sunshine and waller in the shade—
Like the Good Book tells us—"where there're none to make
    afraid!"
Well!—I never seen the ocean ner I never seen the sea.—
On the banks o' Deer Crick's grand enough fer me!

LITTLE ORPHANT ANNIE

Little Orphant Annie's come to our house to stay,
An' wash the cups an' saucers up, an' brush the crumbs away,
An' shoo the chickens off the porch, an' dust the hearth, an'
    sweep,
An' make the fire, an' bake the bread, an' earn her board-an'-
    keep;
An' all us other children, when the supper-things is done,
We set around the kitchen fire an' has the mostest fun
A-list'nin' to the witch-tales 'at Annie tells about,
An' the Gobble-uns 'at gits you
        Ef you
           Don't
              Watch
                Out!

Wunst they wuz a little boy wouldn't say his prayers,—
An when he went to bed at night, away up stairs,
His Mammy heerd him holler, an' his Daddy heerd him bawl,
An' when they turn't the kivvers down, he wuzn't there at all!
An' they seeked him in the rafter-room, an' cubby hole, an'
    press,
An' seeked him up the chimbly-flue, an' ever'wheres, I guess;
But all they ever found wuz thist his pants an' roundabout:—
An' the Gobble-uns'll git you
        Ef you
           Don't
              Watch
                Out!

An' one time a little girl 'ud allus laugh an' grin,
An' make fun of ever'one, an' all her blood an' kin;
An' wunst, when they was "company," an' ole folks wuz there,
She mocked 'em an' shocked 'em, an' said she didn't care!
An' thist as she kicked her heels, an' turn't to run an' hide,
They wuz two great big Black Things a-standin' by her side,

An' they snatched her through the ceilin' 'fore she knowed
  what she's about!
An' the Gobble-uns'll git you
       Ef you
         Don't
           Watch
            Out!

An' little Orphant Annie says, when the blaze is blue,
An' the lamp-wick sputters, an' the wind goes *woo-oo*!
An' you hear the crickets quit, an' the moon is gray,
An' the lighnin'-bugs in dew is all squenched away,—
You better mind yer parunts an' yer teachers fond an' dear,
An' churish them 'at loves you, an' dry the orphant's tear,
An' he'p the pore an' needy ones 'at clusters all about,
Er the Gobble-uns'll git you
       Ef you
         Don't
           Watch
            Out!

THE LAND OF THUS-AND-SO

"How would Willie like to go
To the Land of Thus-and-So?
Everything is proper there—
All the children comb their hair
Smoother than the fur of cats,
Or the nap of high silk hats;
Every face is clean and white
As a lily washed in light;
Never vaguest soil or speck
Found on forehead, throat or neck;
Every little crimpled ear,
In and out, as pure and clear
As the cherry-blossom's blow
In the Land of Thus-and-So.

"Little boys that never fall
Down the stair, or cry at all—
Doing nothing to repent,
Watchful and obedient;
Never hungry, nor in haste—
Tidy shoe-strings always laced;
Never button rudely torn
From its fellows all unworn;
Knickerbockers always new—
Ribbon, tie, and collar, too;
Little watches, worn like men,
Always promptly half-past ten—
Just precisely right, you know,
For the Land of Thus-and-So!

"And the little babies there
Give no one the slightest care—
Nurse has not a thing to do
But be happy and sigh 'Boo!'
While Mamma just nods, and knows

Nothing but to doze and doze:
Never litter round the grate;
Never lunch or dinner late;
Never any household din
Peals without or rings within—
Baby coos nor laughing calls
On the stairs or through the halls—
Just Great Hushes to and fro
Pace the Land of Thus-and-so!

"Oh! the Land of Thus-and-So!
Isn't it delightful, though?"
"Yes," lisped Willie, answering me
Somewhat slow and doubtfully—
"Must be awful nice, but I
Ruther wait till by-and-by
'Fore I go there—maybe when
I be dead I'll go there *then*.—
But"—the troubled little face
Closer pressed in my embrace—
"Le's don't never *ever* go
To the Land of Thus-and-So!"

GRANNY

Granny's come to our house,
   And ho! my lawzy-daisy!
All the children round the place
   Is ist a-runnin' crazy!
Fetched a cake fer little Jake,
   And fetched a pie fer Nanny,
And fetched a pear fer all the pack
   That runs to kiss their Granny!

Lucy Ellen's in her lap,
   And Wade and Silas Walker
Both's a-ridin' on her foot,
   And 'Pollos on the rocker;
And Marthy's twins, from Aunt Marinn's,
   And little Orphant Annie,
All's a-eatin' gingerbread
   And giggle-un at Granny!

Tells us all the fairy tales
   Ever thought er wundered —
And 'bundance o' other stories —
   Bet she knows a hunderd! —
Bob's the one fer "Whittington,"
   And "Golden Locks" fer Fanny!
Hear 'em laugh and clap their hands,
   Listenun' at Granny!

"Jack the Giant-Killer" 's good;
   And "Bean-Stalk" 's another! —
So's the one of "Cinderell'"
   And her old godmother; —
That-un's best of all the rest —
   Bestest one of any, —
Where the mices scampers home
   Like we runs to Granny!

Granny's come to our house,
  Ho! my lawzy-daisy!
All the childern round the place
  Is ist a-runnin' crazy!
Fetched a cake fer little Jake,
  And fetched a pie fer Nanny,
And fetched a pear fer all the pack
  That runs to kiss their Granny!

PAP'S OLD SAYIN'

Pap had one old-fashioned sayin'
  That I'll never quite fergit—
And they's seven growed-up childern
  Of us rickollects it yit!—
Settin' round the dinner-table,
  Talkin' 'bout our friends, perhaps,
Er abusin' of our neghbors,
  I kin hear them words o' Pap's—
    "Shet up, and eat yer vittels!"

Pap he'd never argy with us,
  Ner cut any subject short
Whilse we all kep' clear o' gossip,
  And wuz actin' as we ort:
But ef we'd git out o' order—
  Like sometimes a fambly is,—
Faultin' folks, er one another,
  Then we'd hear that voice o' his—
    "Shet up, and eat yer vittels!"

Wuz no hand hisse'f at talkin'—
  Never hadn't *much* to say,—
Only, as I said, pervidin'
  When we'd rile him thataway:
Then he'd allus lose his temper
  Spite o' fate, and jerk his head
And slam down his case-knife vicious,
  Whilse he glared around and said—
    "Shet up, and eat yer vittels!"

Mind last time 'at Pap was ailin'
  With a misery in his side,
And had hobbled in the kitchen—
  Jes' the day before he died,—
Laury Jane she ups and tells him,

"Pap, you're pale as pale kin be—
Hain't ye 'feared them-air cowcumbers
Hain't good fer ye?" And says he,
    "Shet up, and eat yer vittels!"

Well! I've saw a-many a sorrow,—
    Forty year', through thick and thin;
I've got best,—and I've got *worsted*,
    Time and time and time ag'in!—
But I've met a-many a trouble
    That I hain't run on to twice,
Haltin'-like and thinkin' over
    Them-air words o' Pap's advice:
        "Shet up, and eat yer vittels!"

THE TRAIN-MISSER

At Union Station

'Ll where in the world my eyes has bin —
Ef I hain't missed that train ag'in!
Chuff! and whistle! and toot! and ring!
But blast and blister the dasted train! —
How it does it I can't explain!
Git here thirty-five minutes before
The durn thing's due! — and, drat the thing!
It'll manage to git past — shore!

The more I travel around, the more
I got no sense! — To stand right here
And let it beat me! 'Ll ding my melts!
I got no gumption, ner nothin' else!
Ticket Agent's a dad-burned bore!
Sell you a ticket's all they keer! —
Ticket Agents ort to all be
Prosecuted — and that's jes' what! —

How'd I know which train's fer me?
And how'd I know which train was not?
Goern and comin' and gone astray,
And backin' and switchin' ever'-which-way!
Ef I could jes' sneak round behind
Myse'f, where I could git full swing,
I'd lift my coat, and kick, by jing!
Till I jes' got jerked up and fined! —
Fer here I stood, as a durn fool's apt
To, and let that train jes' chuff and choo
Right apast me — and mouth jes' gapped
Like a blamed old sandwitch warped in two!

GRIGGSBY'S STATION

Pap's got his pattent-right, and rich as all creation;
　But where's the peace and comfort that we all had before?
Le's go a-visitin' back to Griggsby's Station—
　Back where we ust to be so happy and so pore!

The likes of us a-livin' here! It's jest a mortal pity
　To see us in this great big house, with cyarpets on the stairs,
And the pump right in the kitchen! And the city! city! city!—
　And nothin' but the city all around us ever'wheres!

Climb clean above the roof and look from the steeple,
　And never see a robin, nor a beech or ellum tree!
And right here in ear-shot of at least a thousan' people,
　And none that neighbors with us or we want to go and see!

Le's go a-visitin' back to Griggsby's Station—
　Back where the latch-string's a-hangin' from the door,
And ever' neighbor round the place is dear as a relation—
　Back where we ust to be so happy and so pore!

I want to see the Wiggenses, the whole kit-and-bilin',
　A-drivin' up from Shallor Ford to stay the Sunday through;
And I want to see 'em hitchin' at their son-in-law's and pilin'
　Out there at 'Lizy Ellen's like they ust to do!

I want to see the piece-quilts the Jones girls is makin';
　And I want to pester Laury 'bout their freckled hired hand,
And joke her 'bout the widower she come purt' nigh a-takin',
　Till her Pap got his pension 'lowed in time to save his land.

Le's go a-visitin' back to Griggsby's Station—
　Back where they's nothin' aggervatin' any more,
Shet away safe in the woods around the old location—
　Back where we ust to be so happy and so pore!

I want to see Marindy and he'p her with her sewin',
  And hear her talk so lovin' of her man that's dead and gone,
And stand up with Emanuel to show me how he's growin',
  And smile as I have saw her 'fore she putt her mournin' on.

And I want to see the Samples, on the old lower eighty,
  Where John, our oldest boy, he was tuk and burried—for
His own sake and Katy's,—and I want to cry with Katy
  As she reads all his letters over, writ from The War.

What's in all this grand life and high situation,
  And nary pink nor hollyhawk a-bloomin' at the door?—
Le's go a-visitin' back to Griggsby's Station—
  Back where we ust to be so happy and so pore!

KNEE-DEEP IN JUNE

I

Tell you what I like the best—
   'Long about knee-deep in June,
   'Bout the time strawberries melts
On the vine,—some afternoon
Like to jes' git out and rest,
   And not work at nothin' else!

II

Orchard's where I'd ruther be—
Needn't fence it in fer me!—
   Jes' the whole sky overhead,
And the whole airth underneath—
Sorto' so's a man kin breathe
   Like he ort, and kindo' has
Elbow-room to keerlessly
   Sprawl out len'thways on the grass
     Where the shadders thick and soft
   As the kivvers on the bed
   Mother fixes in the loft
Allus, when they's company!

III

Jes' a-sorto' lazin' there—
   S'lazy, 'at you peek and peer
     Through the wavin' leaves above,
     Like a feller 'at's in love
And don't know it, ner don't keer!
Everything you hear and see
   Got some sort o' interest—
   Maybe find a bluebird's nest
   Tucked up there conveenently
   Fer the boy 'at's ap' to be

Up some other apple-tree!
Watch the swallers skootin' past
'Bout as peert as you could ast;
    Er the Bob-white raise and whiz
    Where some other's whistle is.

IV

Ketch a shadder down below,
And look up to find the crow—
Er a hawk,—away up there,
'Pearantly *froze* in the air!—
    Hear the old hen squawk, and squat
    Over ever' chick she's got,
Suddent-like!—and she knows where
    That-air hawk is, well as you!—
    You jes' bet yer life she do!—
        Eyes a-glitterin' like glass,
        Waitin' till he makes a pass!

V

Pee-wees' singin', to express
    My opinion, 's second class,
Yit you'll hear 'em more er less;
    Sapsucks gittin' down to biz,
Weedin' out the lonesomeness;
    Mr. Bluejay, full o' sass,
        In them baseball clothes o' his,
Sportin' round the orchard jes'
Like he owned the premises!
    Sun out in the fields kin sizz,
But flat on yer back, I guess,
    In the shade's where glory is!
That's jes' what I'd like to do
Stiddy fer a year er two!

VI

Plague! ef they ain't somepin' in
Work 'at kindo' goes ag'in'
  My convictions!—'long about
    Here in June especially!—
    Under some old apple-tree,
      Jes' a-restin' through and through
I could git along without
      Nothin' else at all to do
      Only jes' a-wishin' you
Wuz a-gittin' there like me,
And June wuz eternity!

Lay out there and try to see
Jes' how lazy you kin be!—
    Tumble round and souse yer head
In the clover-bloom, er pull
      Yer straw hat acrost yer eyes
      And peek through it at the skies,
    Thinkin' of old chums 'at's dead,
      Maybe, smilin' back at you
In betwixt the beautiful
      Clouds o' gold and white and blue!—
Month a man kin railly love—
June, you know, I'm talkin' of!

VIII

March ain't never nothin' new!—
Aprile's altogether too
  Brash fer me! and May—I jes'
  'Bominate its promiscs,—
Little hints o' sunshine and
Green around the timber-land—
  A few blossoms, and a few
  Chip-birds, and a sprout er two,—
Drap asleep, and it turns in

'Fore daylight and *snows* ag'in!—
But when *June* comes—Clear my th'oat
 With wild honey!—Rench my hair
In the dew! and hold my coat!
  Whoop out loud! and th'ow my hat!—
 June wants me, and I'm to spare!
 Spread them shadders anywhere,
 I'll git down and waller there,
  And obleeged to you at that!

WHEN THE WORLD
BU'STS THROUGH

Casually Suggested by an Earthquake

Where's a boy a-goin',
  An' what's he goin' to do,
An' how's he goin' to do it,
  When the world bu'sts through?
Ma she says "she can't tell
  What we're comin' to!"
An' Pop says "he's ist skeered
  Clean—plum—through!"

S'pose we'd be a-playin'
  Out in the street,
An' the ground 'ud split up
  'Bout forty feet!—
Ma says "she ist knows
  We 'ud tumble in";
An' Pop says "he bets you
  Nen we wouldn't grin!"

S'pose we'd ist be 'tendin'
  Like we had a show,
Down in the stable
  Where we mustn't go,—
Ma says, "The earthquake
  Might make it fall";
An' Pop says, "More'n like
  Swaller barn an' all!"

Landy! ef we both wuz
  Runnin' 'way from school,
Out in the shady woods
  Where it's all so cool!—
Ma says "a big tree

Might sqush our head";
An' Pop says, "Chop 'em out
    Both—killed—dead!"

But where's a boy goin',
    An' what's he goin' to do,
An' how's he goin' to do it,
    Ef the world bu'sts through?
Ma she says "she can't tell
    What we're comin' to!"
An' Pop says "he's ist skeered
    Clean—plum—through!"

THE HAPPY LITTLE CRIPPLE

I'm thist a little cripple boy, an' never goin' to grow
An' git a great big man at all!—'cause Aunty told me so.
When I was thist a baby onc't I falled out of the bed
An' got "The Curv'ture of the Spine"—'at's what the Doctor
    said.
I never had no Mother nen—fer my Pa runned away
An' dassn't come back here no more—'cause he was drunk
    one day
An' stobbed a man in thish-ere town, an' couldn't pay his fine!
An' nen my Ma she died—an' I got "Curv'ture of the Spine"!

I'm nine years old! An' you can't guess how much I weigh, I
    bet!—
Last birthday I weighed thirty-three!—An' I weigh thirty yet!
I'm awful little fer my size—I'm purt' nigh littler nan
Some babies is!—an' neighbors all calls me "The Little Man"!
An' Doc one time he laughed an' said: "I s'pect, first thing you
    know,
You'll have a little spike-tail coat an' travel with a show!"
An' nen I laughed—till I looked round an' Aunty was
    a-cryin'
Sometimes she acts like that, 'cause I got "Curv'ture of the
    Spine"!

I set—while Aunty's washin'—on my little long-leg stool,
An' watch the little boys an' girls a-skippin' by to school;
An' I peck on the winder, an' holler out an' say:
"Who wants to fight The Little Man 'at dares you all to-day?"
An' nen the boys climbs on the fence, an' little girls peeks
    through,
An' they all says: "'Cause you're so big, you think we're 'feard
    o' you!"
An' nen they yell, an' shake their fist at me, like I shake
    mine—
They're thist in fun, you know, 'cause I got "Curv'ture of the
    Spine"!

At evening, when the ironin' 's done, an' Aunty's fixed the fire,
An' filled an' lit the lamp, an' trimmed the wick an' turned it
higher,
An' fetched the wood all in fer night, an' locked the kitchen
door,
An' stuffed the old crack where the wind blows in up through
the floor—
She sets the kittle on the coals, an' biles an' makes the tea,
An' fries the liver an' the mush, an' cooks a egg fer me;
An' sometimes—when I cough so hard—her elderberry wine
Don't go so bad fer little boys with "Curv'ture of the Spine"!

An' nen when she putts me to bed—an' 'fore she does she's
got
My blanket-nighty, 'at she maked, all good an' warm an' hot,
Hunged on the rocker by the fire—she sings me hymns, an'
tells
Me 'bout The Good Man—yes, an' Elves, an' Old Enchanter
spells;
An' tells me more—an' more—an' more!—tel I'm *asleep*, purt'
nigh—
Only I thist set up ag'in an' kiss her when she cry,
A-tellin' on 'bout *some* boy's Angel-mother—an' it's *mine*! . . .
My *Ma's a Angel*—but *I'm* got "The Curv'ture of the Spine"!

But Aunty's all so childish-like on my account, you see,
I'm most afeard she'll be took down—an' 'at's what bothers
me!—
'Cause ef my good old Aunty ever would git sick an' die,
I don't know what she'd do in Heaven—till *I* come, by an'
by:—
Fer she's so ust to all my ways, an' ever'thing, you know,
An' no one there like me, to nurse an' worry over so!—
'Cause all the little childerns there's so straight an' strong an'
fine,
They's nary angel 'bout the place with "Curv'ture of the
Spine"!

OLD OCTOBER

Old October's purt' nigh gone,
And the frosts is comin' on
Little *heavier* every day—
Like our hearts is thataway!
Leaves is changin' overhead
Back from green to gray and red,
Brown and yeller, with their stems
Loosenin' on the oaks and e'ms;
And the balance of the trees
Gittin' balder every breeze—
Like the heads we're scratchin' on!
Old October's purt' nigh gone.

I love Old October so,
I can't bear to see her go—
Seems to me like losin' some
Old-home relative er chum—
'Pears like sort o' settin' by
Some old friend 'at sigh by sigh
Was a-passin' out o' sight
Into everlastin' night!
Hickernuts a feller hears
Rattlin' down is more like tears
Drappin' on the leaves below—
I love Old October so!

Can't tell what it is about
Old October knocks me out!—
I sleep well enough at night—
And the blamedest appetite
Ever mortal man possessed,—
Last thing et, it tastes the best!—
Warnuts, butternuts, pawpaws,
'Iles and limbers up my jaws
Fer raal service, sich as new
Pork, spareribs, and sausage, too.—
Yit, fer all, they's somepin' 'bout
Old October knocks me out!

HER BEAUTIFUL EYES

O her beautiful eyes! they are as blue as the dew
On the violet's bloom when the morning is new,
And the light of their love is the gleam of the sun
O'er the meadows of Spring where the quick shadows run:
As the morn shifts the mists and the clouds from the skies—
So I stand in the dawn of her beautiful eyes.

And her beautiful eyes are as midday to me,
When the lily-bell bends with the weight of the bee,
And the throat of the thrush is apulse in the heat,
And the senses are drugged with the subtle and sweet
And delirious breaths of the air's lullabies—
So I swoon in the noon of her beautiful eyes.

O her beautiful eyes! they have smitten mine own
As a glory glanced down from the glare of The Throne;
And I reel, and I falter and fall, as afar
Fell the shepherds that looked on the mystical Star,
And yet dazed in the tidings that bade them arise—
So I grope through the night of her beautiful eyes.

DOC SIFERS

*Riley endowed his imaginary character Doc Sifers with
many of his father's admirable qualities—particularly his
intense interest in, and talent for, learning new skills and
making things—as well as his broad knowledge of home
remedies.*

Of all the doctors I could cite you to in this-'ere town
Doc Sifers is my favorite, jes' take him up and down!
Count in the Bethel Neighberhood, and Rollins, and Big Bear
And Sifers' standin' jes' as good as ary doctor's there!

There's old Doc Wick, and Glenn, and Hall, and Wurgler, and
    McVeigh,
But I'll buck Sifers 'g'inst 'em all and down 'em any day!
Most old Wick ever knowed, I s'pose, was *whisky*! Wurgler—
    well,
He et morphine—ef actions shows, and facts' reliable!

But Sifers—though he ain't no sot, he's got his faults; and yit
When you *git* Sifers onc't, you've got a *doctor*, don't fergit!
He ain't much at his office, er his house, er anywhere
You'd natchurly think certain fer to ketch the feller there.—

But don't blame Doc: he's got all sorts o' cur'ous notions—as
The feller says, his odd-come-shorts, like smart men mostly
    has.
He'll more'n like be potter'n' 'round the Blacksmith Shop; er
    in
Some back lot, spadin' up the ground, er gradin' it ag'in.

Er at the work bench, planin' things; er buildin' little traps
To ketch birds; galvenizin' rings; er graftin' plums, perhaps.
Make anything! good as the best!—a gun-stock—er a flute;
He whittled out a set o' chesstmen onc't o' laurel root.

Durin' the Army—got his trade o' surgeon there—I own
To-day a finger-ring Doc made out of a Sesesh bone!
An' glued a fiddle onc't fer me—jes' all so busted you
'D 'a' throwed the thing away, but he fixed her as good as new!

And take Doc, now, in *ager*, say, er *biles*, er *rheumatiz*,
And all afflictions thataway, and he's the best they is!
Er janders—milksick—I don't keer—k-yore anything he
    tries—
A abscess; getherin' in yer yeer; er granilated eyes!

There was the Widder Daubenspeck they all give up fer dead;
A blame cowbuncle on her neck, and clean out of her head!
First had this doctor, what's-his-name, from "Pudblesburg,"
    and then
This little red-head, "Burnin' Shame" they call him—Dr.
    Glenn.

And they "consulted" on the case, and claimed she'd haf to
    die,—
I jes' was joggin' by the place, and heerd her dorter cry,
And stops and calls her to the fence; and I-says-I, "Let me
Send Sifers—bet you fifteen cents he'll k-yore her!" "Well,"
    says she,

"Light out!" she says: And, lipp-tee-cut, I loped in town, and
    rid
'Bout two hours more to find him, but I kussed him when I
    did!
He was down at the Gunsmith Shop a-stuffin' birds! Says he,
"My sulky's broke." Says I, "You hop right on and ride with
    me!"

I got him there.—"Well, Aunty, ten days k'yores you," Sifers
    said,
"But what's yer idy livin' when yer jes' as good as dead?"
And there's Dave Banks—jes' back from war without a
    scratch—one day
Got ketched up in a sickle-bar, a reaper runaway.—

His shoulders, arms, and hands and legs jes' sawed in strips!
    And Jake
Dunn starts fer Sifers—feller begs to shoot him fer God-sake.
Doc, 'course, was gone, but he had penned the notice, "At Big
    Bear—
Be back to-morry; Gone to 'tend the Bee Convention there."

But Jake, he tracked him—rid and rode the whole endurin'
    night!
And 'bout the time the roosters crowed they both hove into
    sight.
Doc had to ampitate but 'greed to save Dave's arms, and swore
He could 'a' saved his legs ef he'd be'n there the day before.

Like when his wife's own mother died 'fore Sifers could be
    found,
And all the neighbers fer and wide a' all jes' chasin' round;
Tel finally—I had to laugh—its jes' like Doc, you know,—
Was learnin' fer to telegraph, down at the old deepo.

But all they're faultin' Sifers fer, there's none of 'em kin say
He's biggoty, er keerless, er not posted any way;
He ain't built on the common plan of doctors nowadays,
He's jes' a great, big, brainy man—that's where the trouble
    lays!

THE OLD MAN AND JIM

Old man never had much to say—
   'Ceptin' to Jim,—
And Jim was the wildest boy he had—
   And the old man jes' wrapped up in him!
Never heerd him speak but once
Er twice in my life,—and first time was
When the army broke out, and Jim he went,
The old man backin' him, fer three months;
And all 'at I heerd the old man say
Was, jes' as we turned to start away,—
   "Well, good-by, Jim:
     Take keer of yourse'f!"

'Peared-like, he was more satisfied
   Jes' *lookin'* at Jim
And likin' him all to hisse'f-like, see?—
   'Cause he was jes' wrapped up in him!
And over and over I mind the day
The old man come and stood round in the way
While we was drillin', a-watchin' Jim—
And down at the deepot a-heerin' him say,
   "Well, good-by, Jim:
     Take keer of yourse'f!"

Never was nothin' about the *farm*
   Disting'ished Jim;
Neighbors all ust to wonder why
   The old man 'peared wrapped up in him:
But when Cap. Biggler he writ back
'At Jim was the bravest boy we had
In the whole dern rigiment, white er black,
And his fightin' good as his farmin' bad—
'At he had led, with a bullet clean
Bore through his thigh, and carried the flag
Through the bloodiest battle you ever seen.—

The old man wound up a letter to him
'At Cap. read to us, 'at said: "Tell Jim
    Good-by,
      And take keer of hisse'f!"

Jim come home jes' long enough
   To take the whim
'At he'd like to go back in the calvery—
   And the old man jes' wrapped up in him!
Jim 'lowed 'at he'd had sich luck afore,
Guessed he'd tackle her three years more.
And the old man give him a colt he'd raised,
And follered him over to Camp Ben Wade,
And laid around fer a week er so,
Watchin' Jim on dress-parade—
Tel finally he rid away,
And last he heerd was the old man say,—
   "Well, good-by, Jim:
     Take keer of yourse'f!"

Tuk the papers, the old man did,
   A-watchin' fer Jim—
Fully believin' he'd make his mark
   Some way—jes' wrapped up in him!—
And many a time the word 'u'd come
'At stirred him up like the tap of a drum—
At Petersburg, fer instunce, where
Jim rid right into their cannons there,
And *tuk* 'em, and p'inted 'em t'other way,
And socked it home to the boys in gray,
As they scooted fer timber, and on and on—
Jim a lieutenant and one arm gone,
And the old man's words in his mind all day,—
   "Well, good-by, Jim:
     Take keer of yourse'f!"

Think of a private, now, perhaps,
   We'll say like Jim,
'At's clumb clean up to the shoulder-straps—
   And the old man jes' wrapped up in him!
Think of him—with the war plum' through,
And the glorious old Red-White-and-Blue
A-laughin' the news down over Jim,
And the old man, bendin' over him—
The surgeon turnin' away with tears
'At hadn't leaked fer years and years,
As the hand of the dyin' boy clung to
His father's, the old voice in his ears,—
   "Well, good-by, Jim:
      Take keer of yourse'f!"

WHEN THE GREEN GITS BACK IN THE TREES

In Spring, when the green gits back in the trees,
   And the sun comes out and *stays*,
And yer boots pulls on with a good tight squeeze,
   And you think of yer bare-foot days;
When you *ort* to work and you want to *not*,
   And you and yer wife agrees
It's time to spade up the garden-lot,
    When the green gits back in the trees
      Well! work is the least o' *my* idees
      When the green, you know, gits back in the trees!

When the green gits back in the trees, and bees
   Is a-buzzin' aroun' ag'in
In that kind of a lazy go-as-you-please
   Old gait they bum roun' in;
When the groun's all bald whare the hay-rick stood,
   And the crick's riz, and the breeze
Coaxes the bloom in the old dogwood,
   And the green gits back in the trees,—
     I like, as I say, in sich scenes as these,
     The time when the green gits back in the trees!

When the whole tail-fethers o' Wintertime
   Is all pulled out and gone!
And the sap it thaws and begins to climb,
   And the swet it starts out on
A feller's forred, a-gittin' down
   At the old spring on his knees—
I kindo' like jest a-loaferin' roun'
   When the green gits back in the trees—
     Jest a-potterin' roun' as I—durn—please—
     When the green, you know, gits back in the trees!

DOWN AROUND THE RIVER

Noon-time and June-time, down around the river!
Have to furse with Lizey Ann—but lawzy! I fergive her!
Drives me off the place, and says 'at all 'at she's a-wishin',
Land o' gracious! time'll come I'll git enough o' fishin'!
Little Dave, a-choppin' wood, never 'pears to notice;
Don't know where she's hid his hat, er keerin' where his coat is,—
Specalatin', more'n like, he hain't a-goin' to mind me,
And guessin' where, say twelve o'clock, a feller'd likely find me.

Noon-time and June-time, down around the river!
Clean out o'sight o'home, and skulkin' under kivver
Of the sycamores, jack-oaks, and swamp-ash and ellum—
Idies all so jumbled up, you kin hardly tell 'em!—
Tired, you know, but *lovin'* it, and smilin' jes' to think 'at
Any sweeter tiredness you'd fairly want to *drink* it.
Tired o' fishin'—tired o' fun—line out slack and slacker—
All you want in all the world's a little more tobacker!

Hungry, but *a-hidin'* it, er jes' a-not a-kerrin':—
Kingfisher gittin' up and skootin' out o' hearin';
Snipes on the t'other side, where the County Ditch is,
Wadin' up and down the aidge like they'd rolled their britches!
Old turkle on the root kind o' sort o' drappin'
Intoo th' worter like he don't know how it happen!
Worter, shade and all so mixed, don't know which you'd orter
Say, th' *worter* in the shadder—*shadder* in the *worter*!

Somebody hollerin'—'way around the bend in
Upper Fork—where yer eye kin jes' ketch the endin'
Of the shiney wedge o' wake some muss-rat's a-makin'
With that pesky nose o' his! Then a sniff o' bacon,
Corn-bread and 'dock-greens—and little Dave a-shinnin'
'Crost the rocks and mussel-shells, a-limpin' and a-grinnin',
With yer dinner fer ye, and a blessin' from the giver.
Noon-time and June-time down around the river!

DOWN TO THE CAPITAL

I'be'n down to the Capital at Washington, D. C.,
Where Congress meets and passes on the pensions ort to be
Allowed to old one-legged chaps, like me, 'at sence the war
Don't wear their pants in pairs at all—and yit how proud we
    are!

Old Flukens, from our deestrick, jes' turned in and tuck and
    made
Me stay with him whilse I was there; and longer 'at I stayed
The more I kep' a-wantin' jes' to kind o' git away,
And yit a-feelin' sociabler with Flukens ever' day.

You see I'd got the idy—and I guess most folks agrees—
'At men as rich as him, you know, kin do jes' what they please;
A man worth stacks o' money, and a Congerssman and all,
And livin' in a buildin' bigger'n Masonic Hall!

Now mind, I'm not a-faultin' Fluke—he made his money
    square:
We both was Forty-niners, and both bu'sted gittin' there;
I weakened and onwindlassed, and he stuck and stayed and
    made
His millions; don't know what *I'm* worth untel my pension's
    paid.

But I was goin' to tell you—er a-ruther goin' to try
To tell you how he's livin' now: gas burnin' mighty nigh
In ever' room about the house; and ever' night, about,
Some blame reception goin' on, and money goin' out.

They's people there from all the world—jes' ever' kind 'at
    lives,
Injuns and all! and Senaters, and Ripresentatives;
And girls, you know, jes' dressed in gauze and roses, I *de*clare,
And even old men shamblin' round and a-waltzin' with 'em
    there!

And bands a-tootin' circus-tunes, 'way in some other room
Jes' chokin' full o' hothouse plants and pinies and perfume;
And fountains, squirtin' stiddy all the time; and statutes, made
Out o' puore marble, 'peared-like, sneakin' round there in the
  shade.

And Fluke he coaxed and begged and pled with *me* to take a
  hand
And sashay in amongst 'em—crutch and all, you understand;
But when I said how tired I was, and made fer open air,
He follered, and tel five o'clock we set a-talkin' there.

"My God!" says he—Fluke says to me, "I'm tireder'n you;
Don't putt up yer tobacker tel you give a man a chew.
Set back a leetle furder in the shadder—that'll do;
I'm tireder'n you, old man; I'm tireder'n you.

"You see that-air old dome," says he, "humped up ag'inst the
  sky?
It's grand, first time you see it; but it changes, by and by,
And then it stays jes' thataway—jes' anchored high and dry
Betwixt the sky up yender and the achin' of yer eye.

"Night's purty; not so purty, though, as what it ust to be
When my first wife was livin'. You remember her?" says he.
I nodded-like, and Fluke went on, "I wonder now ef she
Knows where I am—and what I am—and what I ust to be?

"That band in there!—I ust to think 'at music couldn't wear
A feller out the way it does; but that ain't music there—
That's jes' a' *imitation*, and like ever'thing, I swear,
I hear, er see, er tetch, er taste, er tackle anywhere!

"It's all jes' *artificial*, this-'ere high-priced life of ours;
The theory, *it's* sweet enough, tel it saps down and sours.
They's no *home* left, ner *ties* o' home about it. By the powers,
The whole thing's artificialer'n artificial flowers!

"And all I want, and could lay down and *sob* fer, is to know
The homely things of homely life; fer instance, jes' to go
And set down by the kitchen stove—Lord! that 'u'd rest me
    so,—
Jes' set there, like I ust to do, and laugh and joke, you know.

"Jes' set there, like I ust to do," says Fluke, a-startin' in,
'Peared-like, to say the whole thing over to hisse'f ag'in;
Then stopped and turned, and kind o' coughed, and stooped
    and fumbled fer
Somepin' o' 'nuther in the grass—I guess his handkercher.

Well, sence I'm back from Washington, where I left Fluke
    a-still
A-leggin' fer me, heart and soul, on that-air pension bill,
I've half-way struck the notion, when I think o' wealth and
    sich,
They's nothin' much patheticker'n jes' a-bein' rich!

WAITIN' FER THE CAT TO DIE

Lawzy! don't I rickollect
   That-air old swing in the lane!
Right and proper, I expect,
   Old times *can't* come back again;
But I want to state, ef they
Could come back, and I could say
What *my* pick 'ud be, i jing!
I'd say, Gimme the old swing
'Nunder the old locus' trees
On the old place, ef you please! —
Danglin' there with half-shet eye,
Waitin' fer the cat to die!

I'd say, Gimme the old gang
   O' barefooted, hungry, lean,
Ornry boys you want to hang
   When you're growed up twic't as mean!
The old gyarden-patch, the old
Truants, and the stuff we stol'd!
The old stompin'-groun', where we
Wore the grass off, wild and free
As the swoop o' the old swing
Where we ust to climb and cling,
And twist roun', and fight, and lie —
Waitin' fer the cat to die!

'Pears like I most allus could
   Swing the highest of the crowd —
Jes' sail up there tel I stood
   Down-side up, and screech out loud, —
Ketch my breath, and jes' drap back
Fer to let the old swing slack,
Yit my towhead dippin' still
In the green boughs, and the chill
Up my backbone taperin' down,

With my shadder on the groun'
Slow and slower trailin' by—
Waitin' fer the cat to die!

Now my daughter's little Jane's
    Got a kind o' baby-swing
On the porch, so's when it rains
    She kin play there—little thing!
And I'd limped out t'other day
With my old cheer thisaway,
Swingin' *her* and rockin' too,
Thinkin' how *I* ust to do
At *her* age, when suddenly,
"Hey, Gran'pap!" she says to me,
"Why you rock so slow?" . . . Says I,
"Waitin' fer the cat to die!"

THE PET COON

Noey Bixler ketched him, an' fetched him in to me
　　When he's ist a little teenty-weenty baby-coon
'Bout as big as little pups, an' tied him to a tree;
　　An' Pa gived Noey fifty cents, when he come home at noon.
Nen he buyed a chain fer him, an' little collar, too,
　　An' sawed a hole in a' old tub an' turnt it upside down;
An' little feller'd stay in there and won't come out fer you—
　　'Tendin' like he's kind o' skeered o' boys 'at lives in town.

Now he ain't afeard a bit! he's ist so fat an' tame,
　　We on'y chain him up at night, to save the little chicks.
Holler "Greedy! Greedy!" to him, an' he knows his name,
　　An' here he'll come a-waddle-un, up fer any tricks!
He'll climb up my leg, he will, an' waller in my lap,
　　An' poke his little black paws 'way in my pockets where
They's beechnuts, er chinkypins, er any little scrap
　　Of anything 'at's good to eat—an' *he* don't care!

An' he's as spunky as you please, an' don't like dogs at all.—
　　Billy Miller's black-an'-tan tackled him one day,
An' "Greedy" he ist kind o' doubled all up like a ball,
　　An' Billy's dog he gived a yelp er two an' runned away!
An' nen when Billy fighted me, an' hit me with a bone,
　　An' Ma she purt' nigh ketched him as he dodged an'
　　　　skooted through
The fence, she says, "You better let my little boy alone,
　　Er 'Greedy', next he whips yer dog, shall whip you, too!"

THE SQUIRT-GUN UNCLE
MAKED ME

Uncle Sidney, when he was here,
  Maked me a squirt-gun out o' some
Elder-bushes 'at growed out near
Where wuz the brick-yard—'way out clear
    To where the Toll-Gate come!

So when we walked back home again,
  He maked it, out in our woodhouse where
Wuz the old work-bench, an' the old jack-plane,
An' the old 'poke-shave, an' the tools all lay'n'
    Ist like he wants 'em there.

He sawed it first with the old handsaw;
  An' nen he peeled off the bark, an' got
Some glass an' scraped it; an' told 'bout Pa,
When *he* wuz a boy an' fooled his Ma,
    An' the whippin' 'at he caught.

Nen Uncle Sidney, he took an' filed
  A' old arn ramrod; an' one o' the ends
He screwed fast into the vise; an' smiled,
Thinkin', he said, o' when he wuz a child,
    'Fore him an' Pa wuz mens.

He punched out the peth, an' nen he putt
  A plug in the end with a hole notched through;
Nen took the old drawey-knife an' cut
An' maked a hande 'at shoved clean shut
    But ist where yer hand held to.

An' he wropt th'uther end with some string an' white
  Piece o' the sleeve of a' old tored shirt;
An' nen he showed me to hold it tight,
An' suck in the water an' work it right.—
    An' it 'ud ist squirt an' squirt!

OUR HIRED GIRL

Our hired girl, she's 'Lizabuth Ann;
  An' she can cook best things to eat!
She ist puts dough in our pie-pan,
  An' pours in somepin' 'at's good and sweet,
An' nen she salts it all on top
With cinnamon; an' nen she'll stop
  An' stoop an' slide it, ist as slow,
In th' old cook-stove, so's 'twon't slop
  An' git all spilled; nen bakes it, so
  It's custard pie, first thing you know!
    An' nen she'll say:
  "Clear out o' my way!
  They's time fer work, an' time fer play!—
    Take yer dough, an' run, Child; run!
    Er I cain't git no cookin' done!"

When our hired girl 'tends like she's mad,
  An' says folks got to walk the chalk
When *she's* around, er wisht they had,
  I play out on our porch an' talk
To th' Raggedy Man 'at mows our lawn;
An' he says *"Whew!"* an' nen leans on
  His old crook-scythe, and blinks his eyes
An' sniffs all around an' says,—"I swawn!
  Ef my old nose don't tell me lies,
  It 'pears like I smell custard-pies!"
    An' nen *he'll* say,—
  "'Clear out o' my way!
  They's time fer work an' time fer play!
    Take yer dough, an' run, Child; run!
    Er *she* cain't git no cookin' done!'"

Wunst our hired girl, when she
  Got the supper, an' we all et,
An' it wuz night, an' Ma an' me
  An' Pa went wher' the "Social" met,—
An' nen when we come home, an' see
A light in the kitchen-door, an' we
  Heerd a maccordeun, Pa says "Lan'-
O'-Gracious! who can *her* beau be?"
  An' I marched in, an' 'Lizabuth Ann
  Wuz parchin' corn fer the Raggedy Man!
   Better say
"Clear out o' the way!
They's time fer work, an' time fer play!
  Take the hint, an' run, Child; run!
  Er we cain't git no *courtin'* done!"

THE BUMBLEBEE

You better not fool with a Bumblebee!—
Ef you don't think they can sting—you'll see!
They're lazy to look at, an' kindo' go
Buzzin' an' bummin' aroun' so slow,
An' ac' so slouchy an' all fagged out,
Danglin' their legs as they drone about
The hollyhawks 'at they can't climb in
'Ithout ist a-tumble-un out ag'in!
Wunst I watched one climb clean 'way
In a jimpson-blossom, I did, one day,—
An' I ist *grabbed* it—an' nen let go—
An' *"Ooh-ooh! Honey! I told ye so!"*
Says the Raggedy Man; an' he ist run
An' pullt out the stinger, an' don't laugh none,
An' says: "They *has* be'n folks, I guess,
'At thought I wuz predjudust more er less,—
Yit I still muntain 'at a Bumblebee
Wears out his welcome too quick fer me!"

THE RUNAWAY BOY

Wunst I sassed my Pa, an' he
Won't stand that, an' punished me,—
Nen when he wuz gone that day,
I slipped out an' runned away.

I tooked all my copper-cents,
An' clumbed over our back fence
In the jimpson-weeds 'at growed
Ever'where all down the road.

Nen I got out there, an' nen
I runned some—an' runned again,
When I met a man 'at led
A big cow 'at shooked her head.

I went down a long, long lane
Where wuz little pigs a-play'n';
An' a grea'-big pig went "Booh!"
An' jumped up, an' skeered me too.

Nen I scampered past, an' they
Wuz somebody hollered "Hey!"
An' I ist looked ever'where,
An' they wuz nobody there.

I *want* to, but I'm 'fraid to try
To go back. . . . An' by-an'-by,
Somepin' hurts my throat inside—
An' I want my Ma—an' cried.

Nen' a grea'-big girl come through
Where's a gate, an' telled me who
Am I? an' ef I tell where
My home's at she'll show me there.

But I couldn't ist but tell
What's my *name*; an' she says "well,"
An' she tooked me up an' says
"She know where I live, she guess."

Nen she telled me hug wite close
Round her neck!—an' off she goes
Skippin' up the street! An' nen
Purty soon I'm home again.

An' my Ma, when she kissed me,
Kissed the *big girl* too, an' *she*
Kissed me—ef I p'omise *shore*
I won't run away no more!

THE RAGGEDY MAN

O the Raggedy Man! He works fer Pa;
An' he's the goodest man ever you saw!
He comes to our house every day,
An' waters the horses, an' feeds 'em hay;
'An' he opens the shed—an' we all ist laugh
When he drives out our little old wobble-ly calf;
An' nen—ef our hired girl says he can—
He milks the cow fer 'Lizabuth Ann.—
    Ain't he a' awful good Raggedy Man?
      Raggedy! Raggedy! Raggedy Man!

W'y, The Raggedy Man—he's ist so good,
He splits the kindlin' an' chops the wood;
An' nen he spades in our garden, too,
An' does most things 'at *boys* can't do!—
He clumbed clean up in our big tree
An' shooked a' apple down fer me—
An' nother'n', too, fer 'Lizabuth Ann—
An' nother'n', too, fer The Raggedy Man.—
    Ain't he a' awful kind Raggedy Man?
      Raggedy! Raggedy! Raggedy Man!

An' The Raggedy Man one time say he
Pick' roast' rambos from a' orchurd-tree,
An' et em—all ist roast' an' hot!—
An' it's so, too!—'cause a corn-crib got
Afire one time an' all burn' down
On "The Smoot Farm," 'bout four mile from town—
On "The Smoot Farm"! Yes—an' the hired han'
'At worked there nen 'uz The Raggedy Man!—
    Ain't he the beatin'est Raggedy Man?
      Raggedy! Raggedy! Raggedy Man!

The Raggedy Man's so good an' kind
He'll be our "horsey," an' "haw" an' mind
Ever'thing 'at you make him do—
An' won't run off—'less you want him to!
I drived him wunst way down our lane
An' he got skeered, when it 'menced to rain,
An' ist rared up an' squealed and run
Purt' nigh away!—an' it's all in fun!
Nen he skeered *ag'in* at a' old tin can . . .
     Whoa! y' old runaway Raggedy Man!
         Raggedy! Raggedy! Raggedy Man!

An' The Raggedy Man, he knows most rhymes
An' tells 'em, ef I be good, sometimes:
Knows 'bout Giunts, an' Griffuns, an' Elves,
An' the Squidgicum-Squees 'at swallers ther'selves!
An', wite by the pump in our pasture-lot,
He showed me the hole 'at the Wunks is got,
'At lives 'way deep in the ground, an' can·
Turn into me, er 'Lizabuth Ann,
Er Ma er Pa er The Raggedy Man!
   Ain't he a funny old Raggedy Man?
       Raggedy! Raggedy! Raggedy Man!

An' wunst, when The Raggedy Man come late,
An' pigs ist root' thue the garden-gate,
He 'tend like the pigs 'us *bears* an' said,
"Old Bear-shooter'll shoot 'em dead!"
An' race' an' chase' 'em, an' they'd ist run
When he pint his hoe at 'em like it's a gun
An' go "Bang!—Bang!" nen 'tend he stan'
An' load up his gun ag'in! Raggedy Man!
   He's an old Bear-Shooter Raggedy Man!
       Raggedy! Raggedy! Raggedy Man!

An' sometimes The Raggedy Man lets on
We're little *prince*-children, an' old King's gone
To git more money, an' lef' us there—
And *Robbers* is ist thick ever'where;
An' nen—ef we all won't cry, fer *shore*—
The Raggedy Man he'll come and 'splore
The Castul-Halls," an' steal the "gold"—
An' steal *us,* too, an' grab an' hold
An' pack us off to his old "Cave"!—An'
   Haymow's the "cave" o' The Raggedy Man!—
     Raggedy! Raggedy! Raggedy Man!

The Raggedy Man—one time when he
Wus makin' a little bow-n'-orry fer me,
Says "When *you're* big like your Pa is,
Air *you* go' to keep a fine store like his—
An' be a rich merchunt—an' wear fine clothes?—
Er what *air* you go' to be, goodness knows!"
An' nen he laughed at 'Lizabuth Ann,
An' I says "'M go' to be a Raggedy Man!—
   I'm ist go' to be a nice Raggedy Man!"
     Raggedy! Raggedy! Raggedy Man!

THE OLD BAND

*Riley had fond memories of the Greenfield bands. The first
one, the Saxhorn Band, became the regimental band for
Captain Riley's Union cavalry company. After the war
some members of the old band and a group of new musi-
cians, including the three Riley brothers and the three Davis
brothers, formed the Adelphian Band, which later became
the Davis Brothers Band. "The Old Band" was a favorite
of Riley's, and he frequently read it on the lecture platform.*

It's mighty good to git back to the old town, shore,
Considerin' I've be'n away twenty year and more.
Sence I moved then to Kansas, of course I see a change,
A-comin' back, and notice things that's new to me and strange;
Especially at evening when yer new band-fellers meet,
In fancy uniforms and all, and play out on the street—
 . . . What's come of old Bill Lindsey and the Saxhorn
   fellers—say?
   I want to hear the *old* band play.

What's come of Eastman, and Nat Snow? And where's War
   Barnett at?
And Nate and Bony Meek; Bill Hart; Tom Richa'son and that
Air brother of him played the drum as twic't as big as Jim;
And old Hi Kerns, the carpenter—say, what's become o' him?
I make no doubt yer *new band* now's a *competenter* band,
And plays their music more by note than what they play by
   hand,
And stylisher and grander tunes; but somehow—*any*way,
   I want to hear the *old* band play.

Sich tunes as "John Brown's Body" and "Swect Alice," don't
   you know;
And "The Camels Is A-Comin'," and "John Anderson, My Jo";
And a dozent others of 'em—"Number Nine" and "Number
   'Leven"
Was favo-*rites* that fairly made a feller dream o' Heaven.

And when the boys 'u'd saranade, I've laid so still in bed
I've even heerd the locus'-blossoms droppin' on the shed
When "Lily Dale," er "Hazel Dell," had sobbed ·and died
    away—
      . . . I want to hear the *old* band play.

Yer *new* band ma'by beats it, but the *old band's* what I said—
It allus 'peared to kind o' chord with somepin' in my head;
And, whilse I'm no musicianer, when my blame' eyes is jes'
Nigh drownded out, and Mem'ry squares her jaws and sort o'
    says
She *won't* ner *never will* fergit, I want to jes' turn in
And take and light right out o' here and git back West ag'in
And *stay* there, when I git there, where I never haf' to say
    I want to hear the *old* band play.

"COON-DOG WESS"

"Coon-Dog Wess"—he allus went
   'Mongst us here by that-air name.
Moved in this-here Settlement
   From next county—he laid claim,—
Lived down in the bottoms—whare
Ust to be some coons in thare!—

In nigh Clayton's, next the crick,—
   Mind old Billy ust to say
Coons in thare was jest that thick,
   He'p him corn-plant any day!—
And, in rostneer-time, be then
Aggin' him to plant again!

Well,—In Spring o' '67,
   This-here "Coon-dog Wess" he come—
Fetchin' 'long 'bout forty-'leven
   Ornriest-lookin' hounds, I gum!
Ever mortul-man laid eyes
On sence dawn o' Christian skies!

Wife come traipsin' at the rag-
   Tag-and-bobtail of the crowd,
Dogs and children, with a bag
   Corn-meal and some side-meat,—*Proud*
And as *independunt*—*My!*
Yit a mild look in her eye.

Well—this "Coon-dog Wess" he jest
   Moved in that-air little pen
Of a pole-shed, aidgin' west
   On "The Slues o' Death," called then.—
Otter- and mink-hunters ust
To camp thare 'fore game vammoosed.

Abul-bodied man,—and lots
   Call fer *choppers*—and fer hands
To git *cross-ties out.*—But what's
   Work to sich as understands
Ways appinted and is hence
Under speical providence?—

"Coon-dog Wess's" holts was *hounds*
   And *coon-huntin';* and he knowed
His own range, and stayed in bounds
   And left work fer them 'at showed
Talents fer it—same as his.
Gifts regardin' coon-dogs is.

Hounds of ev'ry mungerl breed
   Ever whelped on earth!—Had these
Yeller kind, with punkin-seed
   Marks above theyr eyes—and fleas
Both to sell and keep!—Also
These-here *lop-yeerd* hounds, you know.—

Yes-and *brindle* hounds—and long,
   Ga'nt hounds, with them eyes they' got
So blame *sorry*, it seems wrong,
   'Most, to kick 'em as to not!
Man, though, wouldn't dast, I guess,
Kick a hound fer "Coon-dog Wess"!

'Tended to his own affairs
   Stric'ly;—made no brags,—and yit
You could see 'at them hounds' cares
   'Peared like *his*,—and he'd 'a' fit
Fer 'em, same as wife er child!—
Them facts made folks rickonciled,

Sorto', fer to let him be
   And not pester him. And then
Word begin to spread 'at he

Had brung in as high as ten
Coon-pelts in one night—and yit
Didn't 'pear to boast of it!

Neghborhood made some complaints
    'Bout them plague-gone hounds at night
Howlin' fit to wake the saints,
    Clean from dusk tel plum daylight!
But to "Coon-dog Wess" them-thare
Howls was "music in the air"!

Fetched his pelts to Gilson's Store—
    Newt he shipped fer him, and said,
Sence *he'd* cooned thare, he'd shipped more
    Than three hundred pelts!—"By Ned!
Git shet of my *store*," Newt says,
"I'd go in with 'Coon-dog Wess'!"

And the feller 'peared to be
    Makin' best and most he could
Of his rale prospairity:—
    Bought some household things—and *good*,—
Likewise, wagon-load onc't come
From wherever he'd moved from.

But pore feller's huntin'-days,
    'Bout them times, was glidin' past!—
Goes out onc't one night and *stays*!
    . . . Neghbors they turned out, at last,
Headed by his wife and one
Half-starved hound—and search begun.

Boys said, that blame hound, he led
    Searchin' party, 'bout a half-
Mile ahead, and bellerin', said,
    Worse'n ary yearlin' calf!—
Tel, at last, come fur-off sounds
Like the howl of other hounds.

And-sir, shore enugh, them signs
  Fetched 'em—in a' hour er two—
Whare the *pack* was;—and they finds
  "Coon-dog Wess" *right thare*;—And you
Would admitted he was right
Stayin', as he had, *all night!*

Facts is, cuttin' down a tree,
  The blame thing had sorto' fell
In a twist-like—*mercy me!*
  And had ketched him.—Couldn't tell,
Wess said, *how* he'd managed—yit
He'd got both legs under it!

Fainted and come to, I s'pose,
  'Bout a dozen times whilse they
Chopped him out!—And wife she froze
  To him!—bresh his hair away
And smile cheerful'—only when
He'd faint.—Cry and kiss him *then.*

Had *his* nerve!—And nussed him through,—
  Neghbors he'pped her—all she'd stand.—
Had a loom, and she could do
  Carpet-weavin' railly grand!—
"'Sides," she ust to laugh and say,
"She'd have Wess, now, *night* and day!"

As fer *him*, he'd say, says-ee,
  "I'm resigned to bein' lame:—
They was four coons up that tree,
  And hounds got 'em, jest the same!"
'Peared like, one er two legs less
Never worried "Coon-Dog Wess"!

DECORATION DAY ON THE PLACE

It's lonesome—sorto' lonesome,—it's a *Sund'y-day,* to me,
It 'pears-like—more'n any day I nearly ever see!—
Yit, with the Stars and Stripes above, a-flutterin' in the air,
On ev'ry Soldier's grave I'd love to lay a lily thare.

They say, though, Decoration Days is giner'ly observed
'Most *ev'rywheres*—espeshally by soldier-boys that's served.—
But me and Mother's never went—we seldom git away,—
In p'int o' fact, we're *allus* home on *Decoration Day.*

They say the old boys marches through the streets in colum's
　　grand,
A-follerin' the old war-tunes they're playin' on the band—
And citizuns all jinin' in—and little childern, too—
All marchin', under shelter of the old Red White and Blue.—

With roses! roses! roses!—ev'rybody in the town!—
And crowds o' little girls in white, jest fairly loaded down!—
Oh! don't THE BOYS know it, from theyr camp acrost the
　　hill?—
Don't they see theyr com'ards comin' and the old flag wavin'
　　still?

Oh! can't they hear the bugul and the rattle of the drum?—
Ain't they no way under heavens they can rickollect us some?
Ain't they no way we can coax 'em, through the roses, jest to say
They know that ev'ry day on earth's theyr Decoration Day?

We've tried that—me and Mother,—whare Elias takes his rest,
In the orchurd—in his uniform, and hands acrost his brest,
And the flag he dicd fer, smilin' and a-ripplin' in the breeze
Above his grave—and over that,—*the robin in the trees!*

And *yit* it's lonesome—lonesome!—It's a *Sund'y-day,* to *me,*
It 'pears-like—more'n any day I nearly ever see!—
Still, with the Stars and Stripes above, a-flutterin' in the air,
On ev'ry soldier's grave I'd love to lay a lily thare.

UP AND DOWN OLD BRANDYWINE

Up and down old Brandywine,
  In the days 'at's past and gone—
With a dad-burn hook-and-line
  And a saplin'-pole—i swawn!
    I've had more fun, to the square
    Inch, than ever *any*where!
    Heaven to come can't discount *mine*,
    Up and down old Brandywine!

Hain't no sense in *wishin'*—yit
  Wisht to goodness I *could* jes'
"Gee" the blame' world round and git
  Back to that old happiness!—
    Kind o' drive back in the shade
    "The old Covered Bridge" there laid
    'Crosst the crick, and sort o' soak
    My soul over, hub and spoke!

Honest, now!—it hain't no *dream*
  'At I'm wantin',—but *the fac's*
As they wuz; the same old stream,
  And the same old times, i jacks!—
    Gimme back my bare feet—and
    Stonebruise too!—And scratched and tanned!—
    And let hottest dog-days shine
    Up and down old Brandywine!

In and on betwixt the trees
  'Long the banks, pour down yer noon,
Kind o' curdled with the breeze
  And the yallerhammer's tune;
    And the smokin', chokin' dust
    O' the turnpike at its wusst—
    Saturd'ys, say, when it seems
    Road's jes' jammed with country teams!

Whilse the old town, fur away
  'Crosst the hazy pastur'-land,
Dozed-like in the heat o' day
  Peaceful' as a hired hand.
    Jolt the gravel th'ough the floor
    O' the old bridge!—grind and roar
    With yer blame' percession-line—
    Up and down old Brandywine!

Souse me and my new straw hat
  Off the foot-log!—what *I* care?—
Fist shoved in the crown o' that—
  Like the old Clown ust to wear.—
    Wouldn't swap it fer a' old
    Gin-u-wine raal crown o' gold!—
    Keep yer *King* ef you'll gim-me
    Jes' the boy I ust to be!

Spill my fishin'-worms! er steal
  My best "goggle-eye!"—but you
Can't lay hands on joys I feel
  Nibblin' like they ust to do!
    So, in memory, to-day
    Same old ripple lips away
    At my "cork" and saggin' line,
    Up and down old Brandywine!

There the logs is, round the hill,
  Where "Old Irvin" ust to lift
Out sunfish from daylight till
  Dewfall—'fore he'd leave "The Drift"
    And give *us* a chance—and then
    Kind o' fish back home again,
    Ketchin' 'em jes' left and right
    Where *we* hadn't got "a bite"!

Er, 'way windin' out and in,—
  Old path th'ough the iurnweeds
And dog-fennel to yer chin—
  Then come suddent, th'ough the reeds

And cattails, smack into where
Them-air woods-hogs ust to scare
Us clean 'crosst the County-line,
Up and down old Brandywine!

But the dim roar o' the dam
It 'ud coax us furder still
To'rds the old race, slow and ca'm,
Slidin' on to Huston's mill—
Where, I 'spect, "the Freeport crowd"
Never *warmed* to us er 'lowed
We wuz quite so overly
Welcome as we aimed to be.

Still it 'peared-like ever'thing—
Fur away from home as *there*—
Had more *relish*-like, i jing!—
Fish in stream, er bird in air!
O them rich old bottom-lands,
Past where Cowden's Schoolhouse stands!
Wortermelons—*master-mine!*
Up and down old Brandywine!

And sich pop-paws!—Lumps o' raw
Gold and green,—jes' oozy th'ough
With ripe yaller—like you've saw
Custard-pie with no crust to:
And jes' *gorges* o' wild plums,
Till a feller'd suck his thumbs
Clean up to his elbows! *My!*—
Me some more er lem me die!

Up and down old Brandywine!
Stripe me with pokeberry-juice!—
Flick me with a pizen-vine
And yell "*Yip!*" and lem me loose!
—Old now as I then wuz young,
'F I could sing as I *have* sung,
Song 'ud shorely ring *dee-vine*
Up and down old Brandywine!

THE SCHOOLBOY'S FAVORITE

Over the river and through the wood
  Now Grandmother's cap I spy:
Hurrah for the fun!—Is the pudding done?
  Hurrah for the pumpkin pie!
    —SCHOOL READER.

Fer any boy 'at's little as me,
  Er any little girl,
That-un's the goodest poetry piece
  In any book in the worl'!
An' ef grown-peoples wuz little ag'in
  I bet they'd say so, too,
Ef *they'd* go see *their* old Gran'ma,
  Like our Pa lets *us* do!

Over the river an' through the wood
  Now Gran'mother's cap I spy:
Hurrah fer the fun!—Is the puddin' done?—
  Hurrah fer the punkin-pie!

An' 'll tell *you* why 'at's the goodest piece:—
  'Cause it's ist like *we* go
To *our* Gran'ma's, a-visitun there,
  When our Pa he says so;
An' Ma she fixes my little cape-coat
  An' little fuzz-cap; an' Pa
He tucks me away—an' yells "Hoo-ray!"—
An' whacks Old Gray, an' drives the sleigh
  Fastest you ever saw!

Over the river an' through the wood
  Now Gran'mother's cap I spy:
Hurrah fer the fun!—Is the puddin' done?—
  Hurrah fer the punkin-pie!

An' Pa ist snuggles me 'tween his knees —
   An' I he'p hold the lines,
An' peek out over the buffalo-robe; —
An' the wind ist *blows*! — an' the snow ist *snows*!
   An' the sun ist shines! an' shines! —
An' th' ole horse tosses his head an' coughs
   The frost back in our face, —
An' I'd ruther go to my Gran'ma's
   Than any other place!

Over the river an' through the wood
   Now Gran'mother's cap I spy:
Hurrah fer the fun! — Is the puddin' done? —
   Hurrah fer the punkin-pie!

An' all the peoples they is in town
   Watches us whizzin' past
To go a-visitun our Gran'ma's,
   Like we all went there last; —
But *they* can't go, like ist *our* folks
   An' Johnny an' Lotty, and three
Er four neighber childerns, an' Rober-ut Volney,
   An' Charley an' Maggy an' me!

Over the river an' through the wood
   Now Gran'mother's cap I spy:
Hurrah fer the fun! — Is the puddin' done? —
   Hurrah fer the punkin-pie!

TO ALMON KEEFER

Almon Keefer was a few years older than Riley and read aloud to him, before the poet could read, a book called Tales of the Ocean. *Subtitled "and Essays for the Forecastle, containing matter and incidents HUMOROUS, PATHETIC, ROMANTIC AND SENTIMENTAL," it included chapters titled "Natives Capturing Sailors and Putting Them in Dens of Snakes," "Ghosts of the Sea," "Black Hole of Calcutta," and "Sailors Capturing Monkeys." The book was lost in later years, and Riley searched bookstores for another copy. When at last he found one in Boston in 1895, he wrote this poem on the flyleaf and sent the book to Almon as a Christmas present.*

This first book that I ever knew
Was read aloud to me by you—
Friend of my boyhood, therefore take
It back from me, for old times' sake—
The selfsame "Tales" first read to me,
Under "the old sweet apple tree,"
Ere I myself could read such great
Big words,—but listening all elate,
At your interpreting, until
Brain, heart, and soul were all athrill
With wonder, awe, and sheer excess
Of wildest childish happiness.

So take the book again—forget
All else,—long years, lost hopes, regret;
Sighs for the joys we ne'er attain,
Prayers we have lifted all in vain;
Tears for the faces seen no more,
Once as the roses at the door!
Take the enchanted book—And lo,
On grassy swards of long ago,
Sprawl out again, beneath the shade
The breezy old-home orchard made,
The veriest barefoot boy indeed—
And I will listen as you read.

A PEACE-HYMN OF THE REPUBLIC

*Read by Riley at the 29th Encampment of the Grand Army
of the Republic, which took place at Louisville in 1895.
Riley told Julia Ward Howe that he was inspired by her
"Battle Hymn of the Republic."*

There's a Voice across the Nation like a mighty ocean-hail,
Borne up from out the Southward as the seas before the gale;
Its breath is in the streaming Flag and in the flying sail—
  As we go sailing on.

'Tis a Voice that we remember—ere its summons soothed as
  now—
When it rang in battle-challenge, and we answered vow with
  vow,—
With roar of gun and hiss of sword and crash of prow and
  prow,
   As we went sailing on.

Our hope sank, even as we saw the sun sink faint and far,—
The Ship of State went groping through the blinding smoke
  of War—
Through blackest midnight lurching, all uncheered of moon
  or star,
   Yet sailing —sailing on.

As One who spake the dead awake, with life-blood leaping
  warm—
Who walked the troubled waters, all unscathed, in mortal
  form,—
We felt our Pilot's presence with His hand upon the storm,
   As we went sailing on.

O Voice of passion lulled to peace, this dawning of To-day—
O Voices twain now blent as one, ye sing all fears away,
Since foe and foe are friends, and lo! the Lord, as glad as
  they.—
   He sends us sailing on.

THE HIRED MAN AND FLORETTY

The Hired Man's supper, which he sat before,
In near reach of the wood-box, the stove-door
And one leaf of the kitchen-table, was
Somewhat belated, and in lifted pause
His dexterous knife was balancing a bit
Of fried mush near the port awaiting it.

At the glad children's advent—gladder still
To find *him* there—"Jest tickled fit to kill
To see ye all!" he said, with unctuous cheer.—
"I'm tryin'-like to he'p Floretty here
To git things cleared away and give ye room
Accordin' to yer stren'th. But I p'sume
It's a pore boarder, as the poet says,
That quarrels with his victuals, so I guess
I'll take another wedge o' that-air cake,
Florett', that you're a-*learnin*' how to bake."
He winked and feigned to swallow painfully.—
"Jest 'fore ye all come in, Floretty she
Was boastin' 'bout her *biscuits*—and they *air*
As good—sometimes—as you'll find anywhere.—
But, women gits to braggin' on their *bread*,
I'm s'picious 'bout their *pie*—as Danty said"
This raillery Floretty strangely seemed
To take as compliment, and fairly beamed
With pleasure at it all.
    —"Speakin' *o' bread*—
When she come here to live," The Hired Man said,—
"Never be'n out o' *Freeport* 'fore she come
Up here,—of course she needed '*sperience* some.—
So, one day, when yer Ma was goin' to set
The risin' fer some bread, she sent Florett'
To borry *leaven*, 'crost at Ryans'.—So,
She went and asked fer *twelve*.—She didn't *know*,
But thought, *whatever* 'twuz, that she could keep
One fer *herse'f* she said. O she wuz deep!"

Some little evidence of favor hailed
The Hired Man's humor; but it wholly failed
To touch the serious Susan Loehr, whose air
And thought rebuked them all to listening there
To her brief history of the *city* man
And his pale wife—"A sweeter woman than
She ever saw!"—So Susan testified,—
And so attested all the Loehrs beside.—
So entertaining was the history, that
The Hired Man, in the corner where he sat
In quiet sequestration, shelling corn,
Ceased wholly, listening, with a face forlorn
As Sorrow's own, while Susan, John and Jake
Told of these strangers who had come to make
Some weeks' stay in the town, in hopes to gain
Once more the health the wife had sought in vain:
Their doctor, in the city, used to know
The Loehrs—Dan and Rachel—years ago,—
And so had sent a letter and request
For them to take a kindly interest
In favoring the couple all they could—
To find some home-place for them, if they would,
Among their friends in town. He ended by
A dozen further lines, explaining why
His patient must have change of scene and air—
New faces, and the simple friendships there
With *them*, which might, in time, make her forget
A grief that kept her ever brooding yet
And wholly melancholy and depressed,—
Nor yet could she find sleep by night nor rest
By day, for thinking—thinking—thinking still
Upon a grief beyond the doctor's skill,—
The death of her one little girl.
   "Pore thing!"
Floretty sighed, and with the turkey-wing
Brushed off the stove-hearth softly, and peered in
The kettle of molasses, with her thin
Voice wandering into song unconsciously—
In purest, if most witless, sympathy.—

   " 'Then sleep no more:
     Around thy heart
Some ten-der dream may i-dlee play,
     But mid-night song,
     With mad-jick art,
Will chase that dree muh-way!' "

"That-air besetment of Floretty's," said
The Hired Man, —"*singin*' —she *inhairited*, —
Her *father* wuz addicted—same as her—
To singin'—yes, and played the dulcimer!
But—gittin' back,—I s'pose yer talkin' 'bout
Them *Hammondses*. Well, Hammond he gits out
Pattents on things—inventions-like, I'm told—
And's got more money'n a house could hold!
And yit he can't git up no pattent-right
To do away with *dyin*'.—And he might
Be worth a *million*, but he couldn't find
Nobody sellin' *health* of any kind! . . .
But they's no thing onhandier fer *me*
To use than other people's misery.—
Floretty, hand me that-air skillet there
And lemme git 'er het up, so's them-air
Children kin have their pop-corn."
   It was good
To hear him now, and so the children stood
Closer about him, waiting.
   "Things to *eat*,"
The Hired Man went on, "'smighty hard to beat!
Now, when *I* wuz a boy, we wuz so pore,
My parunts couldn't 'ford pop-corn no more
To pamper *me* with;—so, I hat to go
Without pop-corn—sometimes a *year* er so!—
And *suffer'n' saints*! how hungry I would git
Fer jest one other chance—like this—at it!
Many and many a time I've *dreamp*', at night,
About pop-corn,—all bu'sted open white,
And hot, you know—and jest enough o' salt

And butter on it fer to find no fault—
Oomh!—Well! as I was goin' on to say,—
After a-*dreamin!* of it thataway,
Then havin' to wake up and find it's all
A *dream*, and hain't got no pop-corn at-tall,
Ner hain't *had* none—I'd think, 'Well, *where's the use!*'
And jest lay back and sob the plaster'n' loose!
And I have *prayed*, what*ever* happened, it
'Ud eether be pop-corn er death! . . . And yit
I've noticed—more'n likely so have you—
That things don't happen when you *want* 'em to."
And thus he ran on artlessly, with speech
And work in equal exercise, till each
Tureen and bowl brimmed white. And the he greased
The saucers ready for the wax, and seized
The fragrant-steaming kettle, at a sign
Made by Floretty; and, each child in line,
He led out to the pump—where, in the dim
New coolness of the night, quite near to him
He felt Floretty's presence, fresh and sweet
As . . . dewy night-air after kitchen-heat.

There, still, with loud delight of laugh and jest,
They plied their subtle alchemy with zest—
Till, sudden, high above their tumult, welled
Out of the sitting-room a song which held
Them stilled in some strange rapture, listening
To the sweet blur of voices chorusing:—

       .   .   .   .   .

  "'When twilight approaches the season
    That ever is sacred to song,
Does some one repeat my name over,
    And sigh that I tarry so long?
And is there a chord in the music
    That's missed when my voice is away?—
And a chord in each heart that awakens
    Regret at my wearisome stay-ay—
      Regret at my wearisome stay.'"

All to himself, The Hired Man thought—"Of course
They'll sing *Floretty* homesick!"

    . . . O strange source
Of ecstasy! O mystery of Song!—
To hear the dear old utterance flow along:—

   "'Do they set me a chair near the table
     When evening's home-pleasures are nigh?—.
   When the candles are lit in the parlor,
     And the stars in the calm azure sky.'" . . .

Just then the moonlight sliced the porch slantwise,
And flashed in misty spangles in the eyes
Floretty clenched, while through the dark—"I jing!"
A voice asked, "Where's that song *'you'd* learn to sing
Ef I sent you the *ballat?'*—which I done
Last I was home at Freeport.—S'pose you run
And git it—and we'll all go in to where
They'll know the notes and sing it fer ye there."
And up the darkness of the old stairway
Floretty fled, without a word to say—
Save to herself some whisper muffled by
Her apron, as she wiped her lashes dry.

Returning, with a letter, which she laid
Upon the kitchen-table while she made
A hasty crock of "float,"—poured thence into
A deep glass dish of iridescent hue
And glint and sparkle, with an overflow
Of froth to crown it, foaming white as snow.—
And then—pound-cake, and jelly-cake as rare,
For its delicious complement,—with air
Of Hebe mortalized, she led her van
Of votaries, rounded by The Hired Man.

THE NAME OF OLD GLORY

*Written in 1898. Delivered by Riley at the alumni banquet
that followed his receiving the honorary degree of Doctor of
Letters from the University of Pennsylvania on February
22, 1904.*

I

Old Glory! say, who,
By the ships and the crew,
And the long, blended ranks of the gray and the blue,—
Who gave you, Old Glory, the name that you bear
With such pride everywhere
As you cast yourself free to the rapturous air
And leap out full-length, as we're wanting you to?—
Who gave you that name, with the ring of the same,
And the honor and fame so becoming to you?—
Your stripes stroked in ripples of white and of red,
With your stars at their glittering best overhead—
By day or by night
Their delightfulest light
Laughing down from their little square heaven of blue!—
Who gave you the name of Old Glory?—say, who—
   Who gave you the name of Old Glory?

*The old banner lifted, and faltering then
In vague lisps and whispers fell silent again.*

II

Old Glory,—speak out!—we are asking about
How you happened to "favor" a name, so to say,
That sounds so familiar and careless and gay
As we cheer it and shout in our wild breezy way—
We—the *crowd*, every man of us, calling you that—
We—Tom, Dick, and Harry—each swinging his hat
And hurrahing" Old Glory!" like you were our kin,
When—*Lord!*—we all know we're as common as sin!
And yet it just seems like you *humor* us all
And waft us your thanks, as we hail you and fall

[173]

Into line, with you over us, waving us on
Where our glorified, sanctified betters have gone.—
And this is the reason we're wanting to know—
(And we're wanting it *so!* —
Where our own fathers went we are willing to go.)—
Who gave you the name of Old Glory—Oho!—
    Who gave you the name of Old Glory?

The old flag unfurled with a billowy thrill
For an instant, then wistfully sighed and was still.

III

Old Glory: the story we're wanting to hear
Is what the plain facts of your christening were,—
For your name—just to hear it,
Repeat it, and cheer it, 's a tang to the spirit
As salt as a tear;—
And seeing you fly, and the boys marching by,
There's a shout in the throat and a blur in the eye
And an aching to live for you always—or die,
If, dying, we still keep you waving on high.
And so, by our love
For you, floating above,
And the scars of all wars and the sorrows thereof,
Who gave you the name of Old Glory, and why
    Are we thrilled at the name of Old Glory?

Then the old banner leaped, like a sail in the blast,
And fluttered an audible answer at last. —

IV

And it spake, with a shake of the voice, and it said:—
By the driven snow-white and the living blood-red
Of my bars, and their heaven of stars overhead—
By the symbol conjoined of them all, skyward cast,
As I float from the steeple, or flap at the mast,
Or droop o'er the sod where the long grasses nod,—
My name is as old as the glory of God.
. . . So I came by the name of Old Glory.

THE HIRED MAN'S
FAITH IN CHILDREN

I believe *all* childern's good,
Ef they're only *understood*,—
Even *bad* ones 'pears to me
'S jes' as good as they kin be!

NO BOY KNOWS

*Delivered by Riley at the alumni dinner that followed the
ceremony in which Yale University conferred on Riley the
honorary degree of Master of Arts.*

There are many things that boys may know—
Why this and that are thus and so,—
Who made the world in the dark and lit
The great sun up to lighten it:
Boys know new things every day—
When they study, or when they play,—
When they idle, or sow and reap—
But no boy knows when he goes to sleep.

Boys who listen—or should, at least,—
May know that the round old earth rolls East;—
And know that the ice and the snow and the rain—
Ever repeating their parts again—
Are all just water the sunbeams first
Sip from the earth in their endless thirst,
And pour again till the low streams leap.—
But no boy knows when he goes to sleep.

A boy may know what a long, glad while
It has been to him since the dawn's first smile,
When forth he fared in the realm divine
Of brook-laced woodland and spun-sunshine;—
He may know each call of his truant mates,
And the paths they went,—and the pasture-gates
Of the 'cross-lots home through the dusk so deep.—
But no boy knows when he goes to sleep.

O I have followed me, o'er and o'er,
From the flagrant drowse on the parlor-floor,
To the pleading voice of the mother when
I even doubted I heard it then—
To the sense of a kiss, and a moonlit room,
And dewy odors of locust-bloom—
A sweet white cot—and a cricket's cheep.—
But no boy knows when he goes to sleep.

THE LISPER

Elsie Mingus *lisps*, she does!
She lives wite acrosst from us
   In Miz. Ayers'uz house 'at she
Rents part to the Mingusuz.—
   Yes, an' Elsie plays wiv me.

Elsie lisps so, she can't say
Her own name, ist *anyway!*—
   She says *"Elthy"*—like they wuz
Feathers on her words, an' they
   Ist stick on her tongue like fuzz.

My! she's *purty*, though!—An' when
She *lisps*, w'y, she's purty *nen*!
   When she told me, wunst, her doll
Wuz so "thweet," an' I p'ten'
   I lisp, too,—she laugh'—'at's all!—

She don't never git mad none—
'Cause she know I'm ist in fun.—
   Elsie she ain't one bit sp'iled.—
Of all childerns—ever' one—
   She's the *ladylikest* child!—

My Ma *say* she is! One time
Elsie start to say the rhyme,
   "Thing a thong o' thixpenth"—*Whee*!
I ist *yell*! An' Ma say I'm
   Unpolite as I can be!

Wunst I went wiv Ma to call
On Elsie's Ma, an' eat an' all;
   An' nen Elsie, when we've et,
An' we're playin' in the hall,
   Elsie say: It's etikett

Fer young gentlemens, like me,
Eatin' when they's *company*,
    Not to never ever crowd
Down their food, ner "thip their tea
    Ner thup thoop so awful loud!"

ALMOST BEYOND ENDURANCE

I ain't a-goin' to cry no more no more!
   I'm got ear-ache, an' Ma can't make
      It quit a-tall;
      An' Carlo bite my rubber-ball
   An' puncture it; an' Sis she take
An' poke' my knife down through the stable-floor
      An' loozed it—blame it all!
But I ain't goin' to cry no more no more!

An' Aunt Mame *wrote* she's comin', an' she *can't*—
   Folks is come *there*!—An' I don't care
      She *is* my Aunt!
      An' my eyes stings; an' I'm
      Ist coughin' all the time,
An' hurts me so, an' where my side's so sore
      Grampa felt where, an' he
      Says "Mayby it's *pleurasy*!"
But I ain't goin' to cry no more no more!

An' I clumbed up an' nen falled off the fence,
   An' Herbert he ist laugh at me!
      An' my fi'-cents
It sticked in my tin bank, an' I ist tore
   Purt'-nigh my thumbnail off, a-tryin' to git
   It out—nen *smash* it!—An' it's in there yit!
But I ain't goin' to cry no more no more!

Oo! I'm so wickud!—An' my breath's so *hot*—
   Ist like I run an' don't res' none
But ist run on when I ought to not;
      Yes, an' my chin
   An' lips 's all warpy, an' teeth's so fast,
   An' 's a place in my throat I can't swaller past—
      An' they all hurt so!—
      An' oh, my-oh!
   I'm a-startin' ag'in—
I'm a-*startin'* ag'in, but I *won't*, fer shore!—
I *ist ain't goin' to cry no more no more*!

[180]

WHILE THE HEART BEATS YOUNG!

While the heart beats young!—O the splendor of the Spring,
With all her dewy jewels on, is not so fair a thing!
The fairest, rarest morning of the blossom-time of May
Is not so sweet a season as the season of to-day
While Youth's diviner climate folds and holds us, close ca-
     ressed
As we feel our mothers with us by the touch of face and
     breast;—
Our bare feet in the meadows, and our fancies up among
The airy clouds of morning—while the heart beats young.

While the heart beats young and our pulses leap and dance,
With every day a holiday and life a glad romance,—
We hear the birds with wonder, and with wonder watch their
     flight—
Standing still the more enchanted, both of hearing and of
     sight,
When they have vanished wholly,—for, in fancy, wing-to-wing
We fly to Heaven with them; and, returning, still we sing
The praises of this *lower* Heaven with tireless voice and
     tongue,
Even as the Master sanctions—while the heart beats young.

While the heart beats young!—While the heart beats young!
O green and gold old Earth of ours, with azure overhung
And looped with rainbows!—grant us yet this grassy lap of
     thine—
We would be still thy children, through the shower and the
     shine!
So pray we, lisping, whispering, in childish love and trust,
With our beseeching hands and faces lifted from the dust
By fervor of the poem, all unwritten and unsung,
Thou givest us in answer, while the heart beats young.

BUB SAYS

The moon in the sky is a custard-pie,
   An' the clouds is the cream pour'd o'er it,
   An' all o' the glittering stars in the sky
   Is the powdered sugar for it.

. . . .

Johnts—he's proudest boy in town—
'Cause his Mommy she cut down
His Pa's pants fer Johnts—an' there
Is 'nuff left fer' *nother* pair!

. . . .

One time, when her Ma was gone,
Little Elsie she put on
All her Ma's fine clothes—an' black
Grow-grain-silk, an' sealskin-sack;
Nen while she wuz flouncin' out
In the hall an' round about
Some one knocked, an' Elsie she
Clean forgot an' run to see
Who's there at the door—an' saw
Might quick at wuz her Ma.
But ef she ain't saw at all,
She'd a-knowed her parasol!

. . . .

Gran'pas an' Gran'mas is funniest folks!—
Don't be jolly, ner tell no jokes,
Tell o' the weather an' frost an' snow
O' that cold New Year's o' long ago;
And then they sigh at each other an' cough
An' talk about suddently droppin' off.

'LIZABUTH-ANN ON BAKIN'-DAY

Our Hired Girl, when it's bakin'-day
   She's out o' patience allus,
An' tells us "Hike *outdoors* an' play,
An' when the cookies's done," she'll say,
   "Land sake! she'll come an' call us!"
An' when the little doughbowl's all
Ist heapin'-full, she'll come an' call—
   Nen say, "She ruther take a switchin'
Than have a pack o' pesky children
   Trackin' round the kitchen!"

THE RAGGEDY MAN ON CHILDREN

Children—take 'em as they run—
You kin *bet* on, ev'ry one!—
Treat 'em right and reco'nize
Human souls is all one size.

Jevver think?—the world's best men
Wears the same souls they had when
They run barefoot—'way back where
All these children air.

Heerd a boy, not long ago,
Say his parents *sassed* him so,
He'd *correct* 'em, ef he could,—
Then be good ef *they'd* be good.

SKETCHES
IN PROSE

THE OLD SOLDIER'S STORY

(AS TOLD BEFORE THE NEW ENGLAND SOCIETY IN NEW YORK CITY)

The joke the old soldier tells Riley heard in his boyhood from a circus clown. In 1888 he tried out his version of it on a Louisville audience; "the house went wild and I had to tell it again." Three months later, Mark Twain heard him tell it in Boston and wrote, "In comic-story form the story is not worth the telling. Put into the humorous-story form it takes ten minutes, and is about the funniest thing I ever listened to — as James Whitcomb Riley tells it. He tells it in the character of a dull-witted old farmer who has just heard it for the first time, who is innocent and happy and pleased with himself. . . . at the end of ten minutes the audience have laughed until they are exhausted, and the tears are running down their faces."

Since we have had no stories to-night I will venture, Mr. President, to tell a story that I have heretofore heard at nearly all the banquets I have ever attended. It is a story simply, and you must bear with it kindly. It is a story as told by a friend of us all, who is found in all parts of all countries, who is immoderately fond of a funny story, and who, unfortunately, attempts to tell a funny story himself—one that he has been particularly delighted with. Well, he is not a story-teller, and especially he is not a funny-story-teller. His funny stories, indeed, are oftentimes touchingly pathetic. But to such a story as he tells, being a good-natured man and kindly disposed, we have to listen, because we do not want to wound his feelings by telling him that we have heard it ably told by a great number of people from the time we were children. But, as I say, we cannot hurt his feelings. We cannot stop him. We cannot kill him; and so the story generally proceeds. He selects a very old story always, and generally tells it in about this fashion:—

I heerd an awful funny thing the other day—ha! ha! I don't know whether I kin git it off er not, but, anyhow, I'll tell it to you. Well!—le's see now how the fool-thing goes. Oh, yes!—W'y there was a feller one time—it was durin' the army, and this feller that I started in to tell you about was in the war, and—ha! ha!—there was a big fight a-goin' on, and this feller was in the fight, and it was a big battle and bullets a-flyin' ever' which way, and bombshells a-bu'stin', and cannon-balls a-flyin' 'round promiskus; and this feller right in the midst of it, you know, and all excited and het up, and chargin' away; and the fust thing you know along come a cannon-ball and shot his head off—ha! ha! ha! Hold on here a minute!—no, sir; I'm a-gittin' ahead of my story; no, no; it didn't shoot his *head* off—I'm gittin' the cart before the horse there-shot his *leg* off; that was the way; shot his leg off; and down the poor feller drapped, and of course, in that condition ef somepin' wasn't done fer him he was perfectly he'pless, you know, but yit with presence o' mind enough to know that he was in a dangerous condition ef somepin' wasn't done for him right away. So he seen a comrade a-chargin' by that he knowed, and he hollers to him and called him by name—I disremember now what the feller's name was . . .

Well, that's got nothin' to do with the story, anyway; he hollers to him, he did, and says, "Hello, there", he says to him; "here, I want you to come here and give me a lift; I got my leg shot off, and I want you to pack me back to the rear of the battle"—where the doctors always is, you know, during a fight—and he says, "I want you to pack me back there where I can get med-dy-cinal attention er I'm a dead man, fer I got my leg shot off," he says, "and I want you to pack me back there so's the surgeons kin take keer of me." Well—the feller, as luck would have it, ricko'nized him and run to him and throwed down his own musket, so's he could pick him up; and he stooped down and picked him up and kindo' halfway shouldered him and halfway helt him betwixt his arms like, and then he turned and started back with him—ha! ha! ha! Now, mind, the fight was still a-goin' on—and right at the hot of the fight, and the feller, all excited, you know, like he was, and the soldier that had his leg shot off gittin' kindo' fainty like, and his head kindo' stuck back over the feller's shoulder that was carryin' him. And he hadn't got more'n a couple o' rods with him when another cannon-ball come along and tuk his head off, shore enough!—and the curioust think about it was—ha! ha!—that the feller was a-packin' him didn't know that he had been hit ag'in at all, and back he went—still carryin' the deceased back—ha! ha! ha!—to where the doctors could take keer of him—as he thought. Well, his cap'n happened to see him, and he thought it was a ruther cur'ous p'ceedin's—a soldier carryin' a dead body out o' the fight— don't you see? And so he hollers at him, and he says to the soldier, the cap'n did, he says, "Hullo, there; where you goin' with that thing?" the cap'n said to the soldier who was a-carryin' away the feller that had his leg shot off. Well, his head, too, by that time. So he says, "Where are you goin' with that thing?" the cap'n said to the soldier who was a-carryin' away the feller that had his leg shot off. Well, the soldier he stopped,—kinder halted, you know, like a private soldier will when his presidin' officer speaks to him—and he says to him, "W'y," he says, "Cap, it's a comrade o' mind and the pore feller has got his leg shot off, and I'm a-packin' him back to where the doctors is; and there was nobody to he'p him, and the feller would 'a' died in his tracks—er track ruther—if it hadn't a-been fer me, and I'm a-packin' him back where the surgeons can take keer of him; where he can get medical attendance—er his wife's a widder!" he says, "'cause he's got his leg shot off!" Then *Cap'n* says, "You blame fool you, he's got his *head* shot off." So then the feller slacked his grip on the body and let it slide down to the ground and looked at it a minute, all puzzled, you know, and says, "W'y, he told me it was his leg!" Ha! ha! ha!

WHERE IS MARY ALICE SMITH?

A true story. Mary Alice Smith was the original Little Orphant Annie.

"WHERE—is—Mary—Alice—Smith? Oh—she—has—gone—home!" It was the thin, mysterious voice of little Mary Alice Smith herself that so often queried and responded as above—every word accented with a sweet and eerie intonation, and a very gayety of solemn earnestness that baffled the cunning skill of all childish imitators. A slender wisp of a girl she was, not more than ten years of age in appearance, though it had been given to us as fourteen. The spindle ankles that she so airily flourished from the sparse concealment of a worn and shadowly calico skirt seemed scarce a fraction more in girth than the slim, blue-veined wrists she tossed among the loose and ragged tresses of her yellow hair, as she danced around the room. She was, from the first, an object of curious and most refreshing interest to our family—to us children in particular—an interest, though years and years have interposed to shroud it in the dull dust of forgetfulness, that still remains vivid and bright and beautiful. Whether an orphan child only, or with a father that could thus lightly send her adrift, I do not know now, nor do I care to ask, but I do recall distinctly that on a raw, bleak day in early winter she was brought to us, from a wild country settlement, by a reputed uncle—a gaunt, round-shouldered man, with deep eyes and sallow cheeks and weedy-looking beard, as we curiously watched him from the front window stolidly swinging this little, blue-lipped, red-nosed waif over the muddy wagonwheel to father's arms, like so much country produce. And even as the man resumed his seat upon the thick board laid across the wagon, and sat chewing a straw, with spasmodic noddings of the head, as some brief further conference detained him, I remember mother quickly lifting my sister up from where we stood, folding and holding the little form in unconscious counterpart of father and the little girl without. And how we gathered round her when father brought her in, and mother fixed a cosey chair for her close to the blazing fire, and untied the little summer hat, with its hectic trimmings, together with the dismal green veil that had been bound beneath it round the little, tingling ears. The hollow, pale-blue eyes of the child followed every motion with an alertness that suggested a somewhat suspicious mind.

"Dave gimme that!" she said, her eyes proudly following the hat as mother laid it on the pillow of the bed. "Musn't git it mussed up, sir! er you'll have Dave in yer wool!" she continued, warningly, as our childish interest drew us to a nearer view of the gaudy article in question.

Half awed, we shrank back to our first wonderment, one of us, however, with the bravery to ask: "Who's Dave?"

"Who's Dave?" reiterated the little voice, half scornfully.—"Why, Dave's a great big boy! Dave works on Barnes's place. And he kin purt'-nigh make a full hand, too. Dave's purt'-nigh as tall as your pap! He's purt-nigh growed up— Dave is! And—David—Mason—Jeffries," she continued, jauntily teetering her head from left to right, and for the first time introducing that peculiar deliberation of accent and undulating utterance that we afterward found to be her quaintest and most charming characteristic—"and—David—Mason —Jeffries—he—likes—Mary—Alice—Smith!" And then she broke abruptly into the merriest laughter, and clapped her little palms together till they fairly glowed.

"And who's Mary Alice Smith?" clamored a chorus of merry voices.

The elfish figure straightened haughtily in the chair. Folding the slender arms tightly across her breast, and tilting her wan face back with an imperious air, she exclaimed sententiously, "W'y, Mary Alice Smith is me—that's who Mary Alice Smith is!"

It was not long, however, before her usual bright and infectious humor was restored, and we were soon piloting the little stranger here and there about the house, and laughing at the thousand funny things she said and did. The winding stairway in the hall quite dazed her with delight. Up and down she went a hundred times, it seemed. And she would talk and whisper to herself, and oftentimes would stop and nestle down and rest her pleased face close against a step and pat it softly with her slender hand, peering curiously down at us with half-averted eyes. And she counted them and named them, every one, as she went up and down.

"I'm mighty glad I'm come to live in this-here house," she said.

We asked her why.

"Oh, 'cause," she said, starting up the stairs again by an entirely novel and original method of her own—"'cause Uncle Tomps ner Aunt 'Lizabeth don't live here; and when they ever come here to git their dinners, like they will ef you don't watch out, w'y, then I kin slip out here on these-here stairs and play like I was climbin' up to the Good World where my mother is—that's why!"

Then we hushed our laughter, and asked her where her home was, and what it was like, and why she didn't like her Uncle Tomps and Aunt 'Lizabeth, and if she wouldn't want to visit them sometimes.

"Oh, yes," she artlessly answered in reply to the concluding query; "I'll want to back there lots o' times; but not to see them! I'll—only—go—back—there—to— see"—and here she was holding up the little flared-out fingers of her left hand, and with the index-finger of the right touching their pink tips in ordered notation with the accent of every gleeful word—"I'll—only—go—back—there—to—see— David—Mason—Jeffries—'cause—he's—the—boy—fer —me!" And then she clapped her hands again and laughed in that half-hysterical, half-musical way of hers till we all joined in and made the echoes of the old hall ring again. "And then," she went on, suddenly throwing out an imperative gesture of silence—"and then, after I've been in this-here house a long, long time, and you all git so's you like me awful—awful— awful well, then some day you'll go in that room there—and that room there—and in the kitchen—and out on the porch—and down the cellar—and out in the smoke-house— and the woodhouse—and the loft—and all around—Oh, ever' place—and in here—and up the stairs—and all them rooms up there—and you'll look behind all the doors—and in all the cubboards—and under all the beds—and then you'll look sorry-like, and holler out, kindo' skeert, and you'll say: 'Where—is—Mary—Alice—Smith?' And then you'll wait and listen and hold yer breath; and then somepin'll holler back, away fur off, and say: 'Oh—she—has —gone—home!' And then ever'thing'll be all still ag'in, and you'll be afeared to holler any more—and you dursn't play—and you can't laugh, and yer throat'll thist hurt and hurt, like you been a-eatin' too much calamus-root er somepin'!" And as the little gypsy concluded her weird prophecy, with a final flourish of her big, pale eyes, we glanced furtively at one another's awestruck faces, with a superstitious dread of a vague, indefinite disaster most certainly awaiting us around some shadowy corner of the future. Through all this speech she had been slowly and silently groping up the winding steps, her voice growing fainter and fainter, and the little pixy-form fading, and wholly vanishing at last around the spiral banister of the upper landing. Then down to us from that alien recess came the voice alone, touched with a tone as of wild entreaty and despair: "Where—is—Mary—Alice—Smith?" And the a long, breathless pause, in which our wide-eyed group below huddled still closer, pale and mute. Then—far off and faint and quavering with a tenderness of pathos that dews the eyes of memory even now—came, like a belated echo, the voice all desolate: "Oh—she—has—gone—home!"

What a queer girl she was, and what a fascinating influence she unconsciously exerted over us! We never tired of her presence; but she, deprived of ours by the many household tasks that she herself assumed, so rigidly maintained and deftly executed, seemed always just as happy when alone as when in our boisterous, fun-loving company. Such resources had Mary Alice Smith—such a wonderfully inventive fancy! She could talk to herself—a favorite amusement, I might almost say a popular amusement, of hers, since these monologues at times would involve numberless characters, chipping in from manifold quarters of a wholesale discussion, and querying and exaggerating, agreeing and controverting, till the dishes she was washing would clash and clang excitedly in the general badinage. Loaded with a pyramid of glistening cups and saucers, she would improvise a gallant line of march from the kitchen table to the pantry, heading an imaginary procession, and whistling a fife-tune that would stir your blood. Then she would trippingly return, rippling her rosy fingers up and down the keys of an imaginary portable piano, or stammering flat-soled across the floor, chuffing and tooting like a locomotive. And she would gravely propound to herself the most intricate riddles—ponder thoughtfully and in silence over them—hazard the most ridiculous answers, and laugh derisively at her own affected ignorance. She would guess again and again, and assume the most gleeful surprise upon at last giving the proper answer, and then she would laugh jubilantly, and mockingly scout herself with having given out "a fool-riddle" that she could guess "with both eyes shut."

"Talk about riddles," she said abruptly to us, one evening after supper, as we lingered watching her clearing away the table—"talk about riddles, it—takes—David—Mason— Jeffries—to—tell—riddles! Bet you don't know

> 'Riddle-cum, riddle-cum right!
> Where was I last Saturd'y night?
> The winds did blow—the boughs did shake—
> I saw the hole a fox did make!'"

Again we felt that indefinable thrill never separate from the strange utterance, suggestive always of some dark mystery, and fascinating and holding the childish fancy in complete control.

"Bet you don't know this-'un neether:

> 'A holler-hearted father,
>   And a hump-back mother—
> Three black orphants
>   All born together!'"

We were dumb.

"You can't guess nothin'!" she said, half pityingly. "W'y, them's easy as fallin' off a chunk! First-'un's a man named Fox, and he kilt his wife and chopped her head off, and they was a man named Wright lived in that neighberhood—and he was a-goin' home—and it was Saturd'y night—and he was a-comin' through the big woods—and they was a storm—and Wright he clumb a tree to git out the rain, and while he was up there here come along a man with a dead woman—and a pickaxe, and a spade. And he drug the dead woman under the same tree where Mr. Wright was—so ever' time it 'ud light-nin', w'y, Wright he could look down and see him a-diggin' a grave there to bury the woman in. So Wright he kep' still tel he got her buried all right, you know, and went back home; and then he clumb down and lit out fer town, and waked up the constabul—and he got a supeeny and went out to Fox's place, and had him jerked up 'fore the gran' jury. Then, when Fox was in court and wanted to know where their proof was that he kilt his wife, w'y, Wright he jumps up and says that riddle to the judge and all the neighbers that was there. And so when they got it all studied out—w'y, they tuk old Fox out and hung him under the same tree where he buried Mrs. Fox under. And that's all o' that'n; and the other'n—I promised—David—Mason—Jeffries—I wouldn't—never—tell—no—livin'—soul—'less—he—gimme—leef,—er—they—guessed—it—out—their—own—se'f!" And as she gave this rather ambiguous explanation of the first riddle, with the mysterious comment on the latter in conclusion, she shook her elfin tresses back over her shoulders with a cunning toss of her head and a glimmering twinkle of her pale, bright eyes that somehow reminded us of the fairy godmother in Cinderella.

And Mary Alice Smith was right, too, in her early prog-nostications regarding the visits of her Uncle Tomps and Aunt 'Lizabeth. Many times through the winter they "jest dropped in," as Aunt 'Lizabeth always expressed it, "to see how we was a-gittin' on with Mary Alice." And once, "in court week," dur-ing a prolonged trial in which Uncle Tomps and Aunt 'Lizabeth rather prominently figured, they "jest dropped in" upon us and settled down and dwelt with us for the longest five days and nights we children had ever in our lives experi-enced. Nor was our long term of restraint from childish sports relieved wholly by their absence, since Aunt 'Lizabeth had taken Mary Alice back with them, saying that "a good long visit to her dear old home—pore as it was—would do the child good."

And then it was that we went about the house in moody silence, the question, "Where—is—Mary—Alice—Smith?" forever yearning at our lips for utterance, and the still belated echo in the old hall overhead forever answering, "Oh—she—has—gone—home!"

It was early spring when she returned. And we were looking for her coming, and knew a week beforehand the very day she would arrive—for had not Aunt 'Lizabeth sent special word by Uncle Tomps, who "had come to town to do his millin', and git the latest war news, not to fail to jest drop in and tell us that they was layin' off to send Mary Alice in next Saturd'y."

Our little town, like every other village and metropolis throughout the country at that time, was, to the children at least, a scene of continuous holiday and carnival. The nation's heart was palpitating with the feverish pulse of war, and already the still half-frozen clods of the common highway were beaten into frosty dust by the tread of marshaled men; and the shrill shriek of the fife, and the hoarse boom and jar and rattling patter of the drums stirred every breast with something of that rapturous insanity of which true patriots and heroes can alone be made.

But on that day—when Mary Alice Smith was to return—what was all the gallant tumult of the town to us? I remember how we ran far up the street to welcome her—for afar off we had recognised her elfish face and eager eyes peering expectantly from behind the broad shoulders of a handsome fellow mounted on a great high-stepping horse that neighed and pranced excitedly as we ran skurrying toward them.

"Whoo—ee!" she cried, in perfect ecstasy, as we paused in breathless admiration. "Clear—the—track—there,—old—folks—young—folks!—fer—Mary—Alice—Smith—and—David—Mason—Jeffries—is—come—to—town!"

O what a day that was! And how vain indeed would be the attempt to detail here a tithe of its glory, or our happiness in having back with us our dear little girl, and her hysterical delight in seeing us so warmly welcome to the full love of our childish hearts the great, strong, round-faced, simple-natured "David—Mason—Jeffries"! Long and long ago we had learned to love him as we loved the peasant hero of some fairy tale of Christian Andersen's; but now that he was with us in most wholesome and robust verity, our very souls seemed scampering from our bodies to run to him and be caught up and tossed and swung and dandled in his gentle, giant arms.

All that long delicious morning we were with him. In his tender charge we were permitted to go down among the tumult and the music of the streets, his round, good-humored face and big blue eyes lit with a lustre like our own. And happy little Mary Alice Smith—how proud she was of him! And how closely and how tenderly, through all that golden morning, did the strong brown hand clasp hers! A hundred times at least, as we promenaded thus, she swung her head back jauntily to whisper to us in that old mysterious way of hers that "David—Mason—Jeffries—and—Mary—Alice—Smith—knew—something—that—we—couldn't—guess!" But when he had returned us home, and after dinner had started down the street alone, with little Mary Alice clapping her hands after him above the gate and laughing in a strange new voice, and with the backs of her little, fluttering hands vainly striving to blot out the big teardrops that gathered in her eyes, we vaguely guessed the secret she and David kept. That night at supper-time we knew it fully. He had enlisted.

. . . . .

Among the list of "killed" at Rich Mountain, Va., occurred the name of "Jeffries, David M." We kept it from her while we could. At last she knew.

. . . . .

"It don't seem like no year ago to me!" Over and over she had said these words. The face was very pale and thin, and the eyes so bright—so bright! The kindly hand that smoothed away the little sufferer's hair trembled and dropped tenderly again upon the folded ones beneath the snowy spread.

"Git me out the picture again!"

The trembling hand lifted once more and searched beneath the pillow.

She drew the thin hands up, and, smiling, pressed the pic-

[197]

tured face against her lips. "David—Mason—Jeffries," she said—"le's—me—and—you—go—play—out—on—the—stairs!"

And ever in the empty home a voice goes moaning on and on, and "Where is Mary Alice Smith?" it cries, and "Where—is—Mary—Alice—Smith?" And the still belated echo, through the high depths of the old hall overhead, answers quaveringly back, "Oh—she—has—gone—home!" But her voice—it is silent evermore!

"Oh, Where is Mary Alice Smith?" She taught us how to call her thus—and now she will not answer us! Have we no voice to reach her with? How sweet and pure and glad they were in those old days, as we recall the accents ringing through the hall—the same we vainly cry to her. Her fancies were so quaint—her ways so full of prankish mysteries! We laughed then; now, upon our knees, we wring our lifted hands and gaze, through streaming tears, high up the stair she used to climb in childish glee, to call and answer eerily. And now, no answer anywhere!

How deft the little finger-tips in every task! The hands, how smooth and delicate to lull and soothe! And the strange music of her lips! The very crudeness of their speech made chaster yet the childish thought her guileless utterance had caught from spirit-depths beyond our reach. And so her homely name grew fair and sweet and beautiful to hear, blent with the echoes pealing clear and vibrant up the winding stair: "Where—where is Mary Alice Smith?" She taught us how to call her thus—but oh, she will not answer us! We have no voice to reach her with.

THE OBJECT LESSON

Audiences loved The Object Lesson. *"His triumph in the
number," said Riley's friend Myron Reed, "was largely due
to a* secret laughter *that tickled the poet's soul. He im-
itated a general type of the time, and that was the reason
audiences never failed to recognize it. The Educator was
not confined to out-of-the-way places, but was found in
large cities as well. He was a picturesque donkey and none
enjoyed his caricature more than the teachers."*

Barely a year ago I attended the Friday afternoon exercises of
a country school. My mission there, as I remember, was to
refresh my mind with such material as might be gathered, for
a "valedictory," which, I regret to say, was to be handed down
to posterity under another signature than my own.

There was present, among a host of visitors, a pale young
man of perhaps thirty years, with a tall head and bulging brow
and a highly-intellectual pair of eyes and spectacles. He wore
his hair without roach or "part" and the smile he beamed
about him was "a joy forever." He was an educator—from the
East, I think I heard it rumored—anyway he was introduced
to the school at last, and he bowed, and smiled, and beamed
upon us all, and entertained us after the most delightfully
edifying manner imaginable. And although I may fail to re-
produce the exact substance of his remarks upon that highly
important occasion, I think I can at least present his theme in
all its coherency of detail. Addressing more particularly the
primary department of the school, he said:—

"As the little exercise I am about to introduce is of recent
origin, and the bright, intelligent faces of the pupils before me
seem rife with eager and expectant interest, it will be well for
me, perhaps, to offer by way of preparatory preface, a few
terse words of explanation.

"The Object-Lesson is designed to fill a long-felt want,
and is destined, as I think, to revolutionize, in a great degree,
the educational systems of our land.—In my belief, the
Object-Lesson will supply a want which I may safely say has

heretofore left the most egregious and palpable traces of mental confusion and intellectual inadequacies stamped, as it were, upon the gleaming reasons of the most learned—the highest cultured, and the most eminently gifted and promising of our professors and scientists both at home and abroad.

"Now this deficiency—if it may be so termed—plainly has a beginning; and probing deeply with the bright, clean scalpel of experience we discover that—"As the twig is bent, the tree's inclined." To remedy, then, a deeply-seated error which for so long has rankled at the very root of educational progress throughout the land, many plausible, and we must admit, many helpful theories have been introduced to allay the painful errors resulting from the discrepancy of which we speak: but until now, nothing that seemed wholly to eradicate the defect has been discovered, and that, too, strange as it may seem, is, at last, found emanating, like the mighty river, from the simplest source, but broadening and gathering in force and power as it flows along, until, at last, its grand and mighty current sweeps on in majesty to the vast illimitable ocean of—of—of—Success! Ahem!

"And, now, little boys and girls, that we have had by implication, a clear and comprehensive explanation of the Object-Lesson and its mission, I trust you will give me your undivided attention while I endeavor—in my humble way—to direct your newly acquired knowledge through the proper channel. For instance:—

"This little object I hold in my hand—who will designate it by its proper name? Come, now, let us see who will be the first to answer. 'A peanut,' says the little boy here at my right. Very good—very good! I hold, then, in my hand, a peanut. And now who will tell me, what is the peanut? A very simple question—who will answer? 'Something good to eat,' says the little girl. Yes, 'something good to eat,' but would it not be better to say simply that the peanut is an edible? I think so, yes. The peanut, then, is—an edible—now, all together, an edible!

"To what kingdom does the peanut belong? The animal, vegetable or mineral kingdom? A very easy question. Come, let us have prompt answers. 'The animal kingdom,' does the little boy say? Oh, no! The peanut does not belong to the animal kingdom! Surely the little boy must be thinking of a larger object than the peanut—the elephant, perhaps. To what kingdom, then, does the peanut belong? The v-v-veg—'The vegetable kingdom,' says the bright-faced little girl on the back seat. Ah! that is better. We find then that the peanut belongs to the—what kingdom? The 'vegetable kingdom.' Very good, very good!

"And now who will tell us of what the peanut is composed. Let us have quick responses now. Time is fleeting! Of what is the peanut composed? 'The hull and the goody,' some one answers. Yes, 'the hull and the goody' in vulgar parlance, but how much better it would be to say simply, the shell and the kernel. Would not that sound better? Yes, I thought you would agree with me there!

"And now who will tell me the color of the peanut! And be careful now! for I shouldn't like to hear you make the very stupid blunder I once heard a little boy make in reply to the same question. Would you like to hear what color the stupid little boy said the peanut was? You would, eh? Well, now, how many of you would like to hear what color the stupid little boy said the peanut was? Come now, let's have an expression. All who would like to hear what color the stupid little boy said the peanut was, may hold up their right hands. Very good, very good—there, that will do.

"Well, it was during a professional visit I was once called upon to make to a neighboring city, where I was invited to address the children of a free school—Hands down, now, little boy—founded for the exclusive benefit of the little newsboys and bootblacks, who, it seems, had not the means to defray the expenses of the commonest educational accessories, and during an object lesson identical with the one before us now—for it is a favorite one of mine—I propounded the question, what is the color of the peanut? Many answers were given in response, but none as sufficiently succinct and apropos as I deemed the facts demanded; and so at last I personally addressed a ragged, but, as I then thought, a bright-eyed little fellow, when judge of my surprise, in reply to my question, what is the color of a of a peanut, the little fellow, without the slightest gleam of intelligence lighting up his face, answered, that 'if not scorched by roasting, the peanut was a blond.' Why, I was almost tempted to join in the general merriment his inapposite reply elicited. But I occupy your attention with trivial things; and as I notice the time allotted me has slipped away, we will drop the peanut for the present. Trusting the few facts gleaned from a topic so homely and unpromising will sink deep in your minds, in time to bloom and blossom in the fields of future usefulness—I—I—I thank you."